SRI YANTRA

with
Golden Ratio Triangle
and
Inscriptions

भावनोपनिषद् (श्रीचक्रोपनिषद्)

Contains original verses from the Bhavana Upanishad of Atharvaveda

Ashwini Kumar Aggarwal

जय गुरुदेव

ISBN13: 978-93-95766-54-8 Paperback Edition
ISBN13: 978-93-95766-55-5 Hardbound Edition
ISBN13: 978-93-95766-52-4 Digital Edition

Title: **Sri Yantra with Golden Ratio Triangle and Inscriptions**
Author: **Ashwini Kumar Aggarwal**

Printed and Published by
Devotees of Sri Sri Ravi Shankar Ashram
34 Sunny Enclave, Devigarh Road,
Patiala 147001, Punjab, India

https://advaita56.in/
The Art of Living Centre

https://www.artofliving.org/

4th June 2023 Sunday, IIT Advanced Exam Havan, Kabir Jayanti, Jyeshtha Masa, Ganges bath Poornima, Sarvartha Siddhi Yoga, Jyeshtha Nakshatra, Grishma Ritu, Uttarayana.

On this day in 781BC 1st written record of solar eclipse, 1783 Montgolfier brothers 1st hot air Balloon flight, 1876 World's 1st transcontinental Train reaches San Francisco from New York, 1887 Pasteur Institute founded in Paris, 1896 Ford unveils world's 1st Automobile, 1917 1st Pulitzer Prize awarded, 1964 Beatles 1st world tour begins, 1969 Man survives 9 hours flight hidden in wheel well of aircraft at temp -40°, 1974 Sally Murphy is world's 1st female aviator.

Vikram Samvat 2080 Pingala, Saka Era 1945 Shobhakrit

1st Edition June 2023

जय गुरुदेव

Dedication

Sri Sri Ravi Shankar

who gave us **Devi Puja sacred geometry** in the form of **Navratri Chandi Homa structures**

Acknowledgements

Project planning for Sunview Enclave Residency main square, Installation of Sri Yantra. April 2023.

Blessing

All the Saints in the past, when they went deep into meditation, they just heard Om. So, Om means many things. It means love, eternity, purity, peace. Om is made up of several dhatus: 'Ah' 'Oo' 'Ma'. Just 'Ah' has 19 meanings.

The total prana is represented by one syllable OM. Before birth, we were part of that sound and after death we will merge with that sound; the SOUND of the Spirit.

Sri Sri Ravi Shankar
Birthday Celebrations, Montreal
Q & A in Canadian Ashram, May 10, 2012

Prayer

ॐ

भद्रं कर्णेभिः श्रृणुयाम देवाः । भद्रं पश्येम आक्षभिर्यजत्राः ।

स्थिरैरङ्गैस्तुष्टुवाꣳसस्तनूभिः । व्यशेम देवहितं यदायुः ॥

स्वस्ति न इन्द्रो वृद्धश्रवाः । स्वस्ति नः पूषा विश्ववेदाः ।

स्वस्ति नस्ताक्ष्र्यो अरिष्टनेमिः । स्वस्ति नो बृहस्पतिर्दधातु ॥

ॐ शान्तिः शान्तिः शान्तिः ॥

Shanti Mantra of Atharvaveda

O Divine Wisdom!
May our ears listen to the sacred and the auspicious.
May our eyes see the propitious as we come together to partake of wisdom.
May our limbs be firm and body attuned to long endurances.
May our senses function with full alertness and
May the sense of contentment be strong.
May our good thoughts form a discus to shield us, and
May our education give us a shining personality.

Peace in our heart, in our body and in our environs.

Contents

Preface

What is a Sri Yantra? A healing mandala diagram made by 4 Upward Apex Triangles and 5 Downward Apex Triangles, properly intertwined to represent

- the cosmic forces in creation, and
- the principles of duality, harmony, and divinity.

The 9 Basic Triangles create a total of 43 Triangles due to the overlapping, which are grouped (shaded) as 14 + 10 + 10 + 8 + 1 = 43.

Apart from these Triangles,

- there is a central Dot (Bindu)
- there are three Circles encircling the Triangles
- there are four Gates encircling the entire Mandala, composed of three lines.

Sanskrit Seed Sounds (bija mantra) like ॐ Om, are potent healing and nourishing energies. Sound is an energy. Pleasing sounds (meditative music, blessings) have excellent effects on one's behavior, attitude, and long-term all round success in life. Harsh and deterring sounds (cruel speech, improper audio-video) wipe away our enthusiasm, drain our energy, block talent and result in suffocation and clouding of neural activity, thereby reducing success.

An aesthetically made Mandala can become vastly superior when infused with Seed Sounds. It is like getting a good vehicle and then employing a proper driver. The Sri Yantra is one of the most ancient mystical, benevolent and highly rewarding mathematical forms of sacred geometry. Recent archaeological and scientific explorations have again and again highlighted that famous and affluent cities of the world e g , Washington DC, Paris, Bombay, etc. have been built using principles of sacred geometry. Architects and Engineers like Leonardo Da Vinci, Mayan Vishwakarma, etc.; and Structures including the Great Pyramid of Giza, the Taj Mahal, the Shiva Shakti temples of Thanjavur, etc.; have made extensive use of sacred geometry.

This book contains the procedure to draw a Sri Yantra using an engineering software like AutoCAD. It is hoped that modern architects, builders and Yantra manufacturers can employ precise techniques to get it right.

Introduction

Avaranas - the nine enclosures, and their Sanskrit Alphabet Letters, i.e., Seed Sounds.

नव आवरण A discussion and drawing of the Nine Enclosures is given herein.

There are principally three historical texts that throw light on this topic.
  a) Bhavana Upanishad (Bhavanopanishad) from Atharvaveda
  b) Soundaraya Lahiri of Adi Shankaracharya
  c) Sri Matrika Chakra Viveka of Kashmir Shaivism

We have taken the commentary of Bhavana Upanishad for this book.

At the end, the slightly alternate view from Sri Matrika Chakra Viveka is also given.

1. त्रैलोक्यमोहन चक्रं that which attracts, impresses and infatuates all the three worlds

2. सर्व आशापरिपूरक चक्रं that which fulfills desires and needs of all

3. सर्व संक्षोभण चक्रं that which attracts, impresses and infatuates all the three worlds

4. सर्व सौभाग्यदायक चक्रं that which proves to be fortunate for all

5. सर्वार्थसाधक चक्रं that which provides for and nourishes all

6. सर्व रक्षाकर चक्रं that which protects and guards all

7. सर्व रोगहर चक्रं that which banishes illness and grief from all

8. सर्व सिद्धिप्रद चक्रं that which enhances the talents of each and blossoms everyone

9. सर्व आनन्दमय चक्रं that which infuses bliss, the pure undiluted joy in everyone

Directions in a Sri Yantra

In the Sri Yantra, we travel **anticlockwise** since East is depicted below. Sequence is:
i.East ii.NorthEast iii.North iv.NorthWest v.West vi.SouthWest vii.South viii.SouthEast

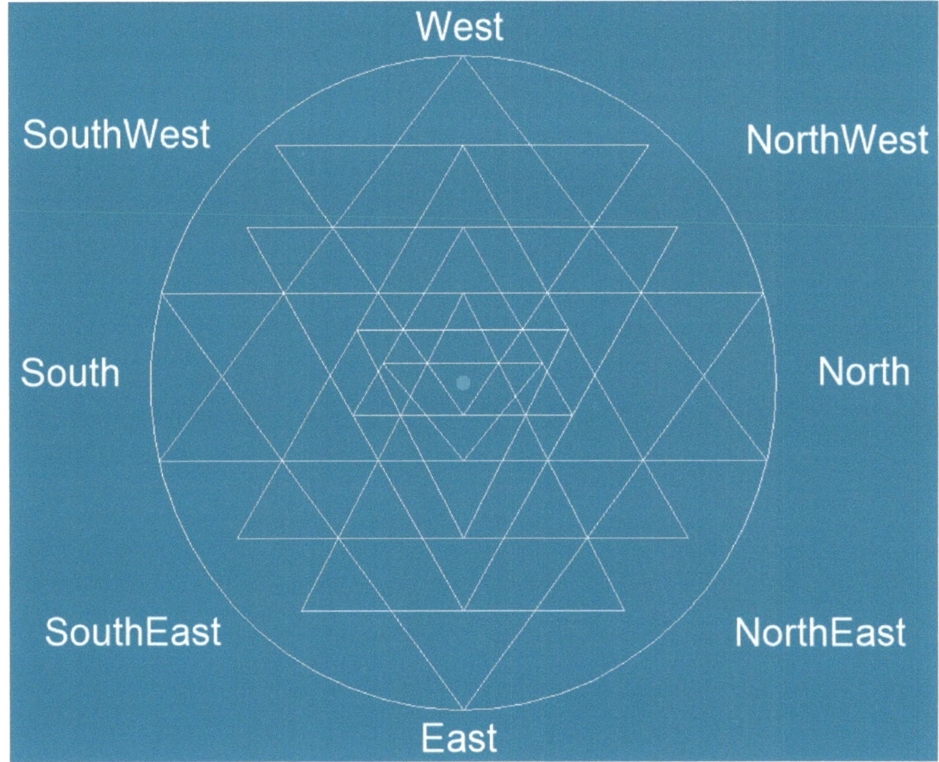

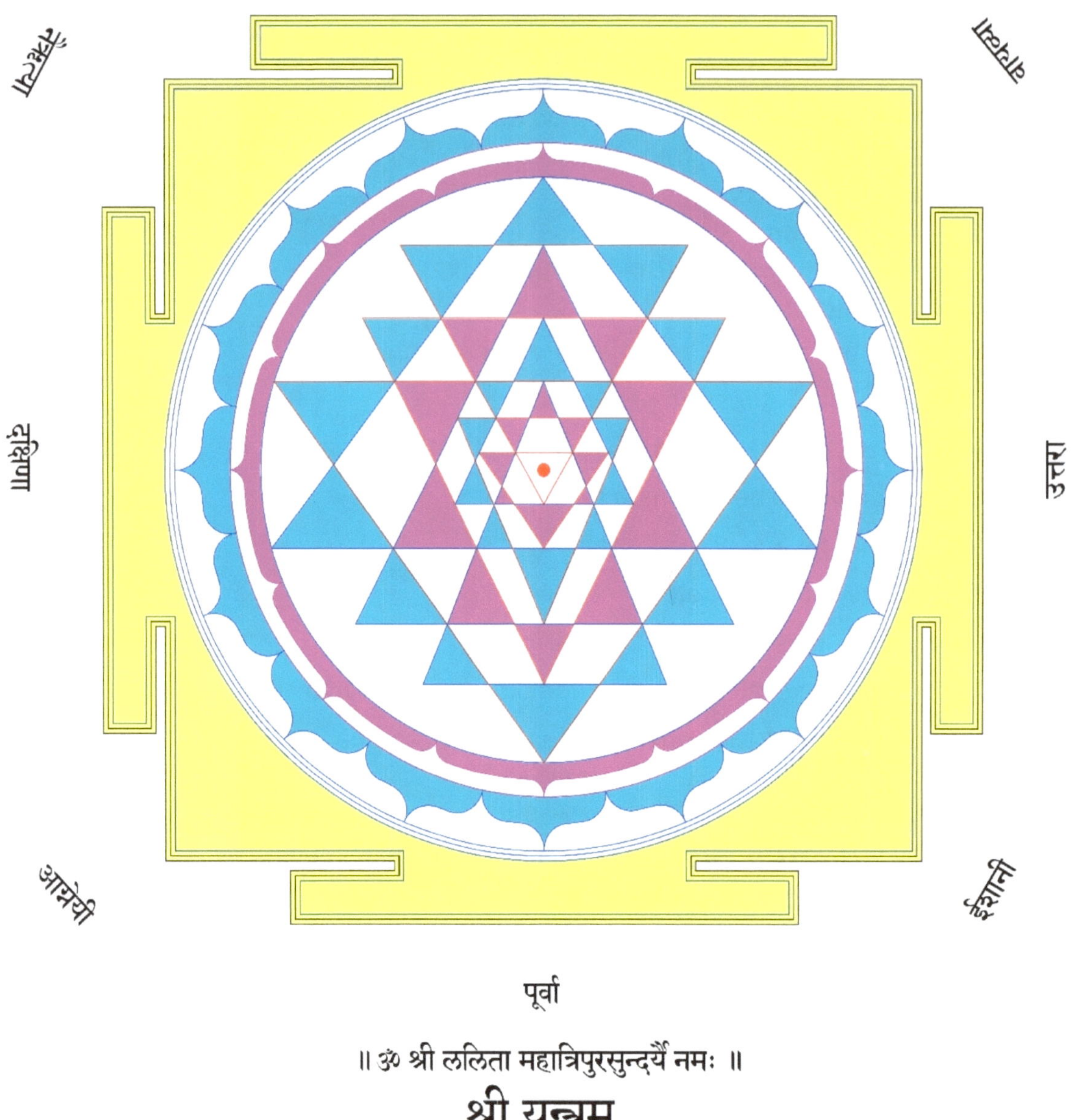

॥ ॐ श्री ललिता महात्रिपुरसुन्दर्यै नमः ॥

श्री यन्त्रम्

In Sanskrit we use the **feminine** spellings for the directions and the divinities.
पूर्वा, ईशानी, उत्तरा, वायव्या, पश्चिमा, नैर्ऋत्या, दक्षिणा, आग्नेयी ।

पूर्वा East, ईशानी NorthEast, उत्तरा North, वायव्या NorthWest, पश्चिमा West, नैर्ऋत्या SouthWest, दक्षिणा South, आग्नेयी SouthEast.

Bhavana Upanishad Verses - Bhāvanopaniṣad भावनोपनिषद्

The Bhavanopanishad is attributed to the Atharvaveda. It expounds the innermost intense feelings of the Soul, its basic desire, and ways and means to connect and unite with the ultimate consciousness.

ॐ भद्रं कर्णेभिः शृणुयाम देवाः । भद्रं पश्ये माक्षभिर् यजत्राः । स्थिरैरङ्गैस् तुष्टुवां सस्तनूभिः । व्यशेम देवहितं यदायुः ॥

स्वस्ति न इन्द्रो वृद्धश्रवाः । स्वस्ति नः पूषा विश्ववेदाः । स्वस्ति नस्ताक्ष्र्यो अरिष्टनेमिः । स्वस्ति नो बृहस्पतिर्दधातु ॥

ॐ शान्तिः शान्तिः शान्तिः ॥

ॐ आत्मानम् अखण्ड-मण्डलाकारम् आवृत्य सकल-ब्रह्माण्ड-मण्डलं स्वप्रकाशं ध्यायेत् । श्री गुरुः सर्वकारणभूता शक्तिः ॥ १ ॥

तेन नव-रन्ध्र-रूपो देहः ॥ २ ॥ नव-शक्ति-रूपश् श्री-चक्रम् ॥ ३ ॥ वाराही पितृरूपा । कुरुकुल्ला बलिदेवता माता ॥ ४ ॥

पुरुषार्थाः सागराः ॥ ५ ॥ देहो नव-रत्न-द्वीपः ॥ ६ ॥ त्वक्-आदि-सप्त-धातुभिः अनेकैः संयुक्ताः सङ्कल्पाः कल्पतरवः ॥ ७ ॥

तेजः कल्पक-उद्यानम् ॥ ८ ॥ रसनया भाव्यमाना मधुः-आम्ल-तिक्त-कटु-कषाय-लवण-रसाः षड् ऋतवः । क्रिया-शक्तिः पीठम् ।

कुण्डलिनी ज्ञान-शक्तिः गृहम् । इच्छा-शक्तिः महात्रिपुरसुन्दरी ॥ ९ ॥

ज्ञाता होता ज्ञानम् अग्निः ज्ञेयश् हविः । ज्ञातृ-ज्ञान-ज्ञेयानाम् अभेदभावनश् श्री-चक्र-पूजनम् ॥ १० ॥

<u>Enclosures</u>

1st. नियति सहिताः शृङ्गाः आद्यो नव-रसाः अणिमा आदयः । काम-क्रोध-लोभ-मोह-मद-मात्सर्य-पुण्य-पापमय्यी ब्राह्मि आदि अष्ट शक्तयः ॥ ११ ॥ आधर-नवकं मुद्रा-शक्तयः ॥ १२ ॥

2nd. पृथिवी-अप-तेजः-वायु-आकाश-श्रोत्र-त्वक्-चक्षुः-जिह्वा-घ्राण-वाक्-पाणि-पाद-पायु-उपस्थ-मनोविकाराः कामाकर्षिणी आदि षोडश शक्तयः ॥ १३ ॥

3rd. वचन-आदान-गमन-विसर्ग-आनन्द-हान-उपादान-उपेक्षा-बुद्धयः अन्-अङ्ग-कुसुमा आदि शक्तयः अष्टौ ॥ १४ ॥

4th. अलम्बुषा कुहूः विश्वोदरा वारणा हस्तिजिह्वा यशोवती पयस्विनी गान्धारी पूषा शङ्खिनी सरस्वती इडा पिङ्गला सुषुम्ना चेति चतुर्दशः नाड्यः । सर्व-संक्षोभिणी आदि चतुर्दशारगा देवताः ॥ १५ ॥

5th. प्राण-अपान-व्यान-उदान-समान-नाग-कूर्म-कृकर-देवदत्त-धनञ्जयाः इति दशावायवः । सर्व-सिद्धिप्रदा देव्यो बहिर्दशारगा देवताः ॥१६

6th. एतद् वायु-दशक संसर्गोपाधिभेदेन रेचक-पाचक-शोषक-दाहक-प्लावकाः अमृतमिति प्राणमुख्यत्वेन पञ्चधा जठर-अग्निः भवति ॥१७

क्षारकः उद्धारकः क्षोभकः मोहकः जृम्भकः इति नाग-प्राधान्येन पञ्चविधोऽस्ति । तेन मनुष्याणां देहानां भक्ष्य-भोज्य-चोष्य-लेह्य-पेयात्मकं पञ्चविधम्-अन्नं पाचयन्ति ॥ १८ ॥ एता दश वह्निकलाः सर्वज्ञाद्याः अन्तर्दशारगा देवताः ॥ १९ ॥

7th. शीत-उष्ण-सुख-दुःख-इच्छाः सत्त्व-रजस्-तमोगुणाः वशिनी आदि शक्तयः अष्टौ ॥ २० ॥

8th. शब्द-स्पर्श-रूप-रस-गन्धाः पञ्च-तन्मात्राः पञ्च-पुष्पबाणाः ॥२१॥ मनः इक्षु-धनुः ॥२२॥ रागः पाशः ॥२३॥ द्वेषः अङ्कुशः ॥२४

अव्यक्त-महत्तत्त्वम्-महत्अहङ्काराः इति कामेश्वरी-वज्रेश्वरी-भगमालिनी अन्तस् त्रिकोण-अग्रगा देवताः ॥ २५ ॥

9th. निरुपाधिका संविदेव कामेश्वरः ॥ २६ ॥ सदानन्दपूर्णा स्वात्मैव परदेवता ललिता ॥ २७ ॥ लौहित्यमेतस्य सर्वस्य विमर्शः ॥ २८॥

अनन्यचित्तत्वेन च सिद्धिः ॥ २९॥ भावनायाः क्रियाः उपचाराः ॥ ३० ॥ अहं त्वम् अस्ति नास्ति कर्तव्यम् अकर्तव्यम् उपासितव्यम् इति विकल्पानाम् आत्मनि विलापनं होमः ॥ ३१॥ भावना विषयाणाम् अभेद-भावना तर्पणम् ॥ ३२॥ पञ्चदश तिथि-रूपेण कालस्य परिणामा अवलोकनं पञ्चदश नित्याः ॥ ३३॥ एवं मुहूर्त-त्रितयं मुहूर्त-द्वितयं मुहूर्त-मात्रं वा भावनापरो जीवन्मुक्तो भवति । स एव शिवयोगी इति कथ्यते ॥ ३४॥ कादिमतेन अन्तश्चक्र-भावनाः प्रतिपादिताः ॥ ३५॥ य एवं वेद । सः अथर्वशिरः अधीते ॥ ३६॥

इत्युपनिषत् ॥

ॐ भद्रं कर्णेभिः शृणुयाम देवाः । भद्रं पश्ये माक्षभिर् यजत्राः । स्थिरैरङ्गैस् तुष्टुवां सस्तनूभिः । व्यशेम देवहितं यदायुः ॥ स्वस्ति न इन्द्रो वृद्धश्रवाः । स्वस्ति नः पूषा विश्ववेदाः । स्वस्ति नस्ताक्ष्र्यो अरिष्टनेमिः । स्वस्ति नो बृहस्पतिर्दधातु ॥ ॐ शान्तिः शान्तिः शान्तिः ॥

॥ ॐ श्री ललिता महात्रिपुरसुन्दर्यै नमः ॥

श्री यन्त्रम्

1st Enclosure Prathamā Āvaraṇa – Four Square Gates

नियति सहिताः शृङ्गाः आदयो नव-रसाः अणिमा आदयः । काम-क्रोध-लोभ-मोह-मद-मात्सर्य-पुण्य-पापमय्यी ब्राह्मि आदि अष्ट शक्तयः ॥ ११ ॥ आधर-नवकं मुद्रा-शक्तयः ॥ १२ ॥

niyati sahitāḥ śaṛṅgāḥ ādayo nava-rasāḥ aṇimā ādayaḥ | kāma-krodha-lobha-moha-mada-mātsarya-puṇya-pāpamayyī brāhmi ādi aṣṭa śaktayaḥ ‖ 11 ‖ ādhara-navakaṃ mudrā-śaktayaḥ ‖ 12 ‖

Linked to mankind's hope and destiny and evolution,
- the 9 emotions of the heart, Perfection etc., are named as Anima etc., respectively. Anima is the term for miniscule, tiny, atomic. These 9 constitute the siddhis that humans aspire for.

Desire, Anger, Greed, Infatuation, Pride, Envy, Meritorious deeds, and Improper deeds due to weakness; constitute the 8 responses, named Brahmi etc.
- theses 8 responses of man are governed by divinities named Brahmi etc.

The 9 apertures in a human body point towards the proper posture.
- Proper posture is a must so that the 9 openings in the body can function normally and give man appropriate strength and power in day to day activity.

1st avarana प्रथम-आवरणम् = श्री त्रैलोक्य मोहन चक्रं

We start from East bottom and move clockwise. Consists of 10 siddhis.

E   01 अं अणिमा सिद्धौ नमः ॥
S   02 मं महिमा सिद्धौ नमः ॥
W   03 लं लघिमा सिद्धौ नमः ॥
N   04 ई ईशित्व सिद्धौ नमः ॥
SE 05 वं वशित्व सिद्धौ नमः ॥
SW 06 पं प्राकाम्य सिद्धौ नमः ॥
NW 07 भुं भुक्ति सिद्धौ नमः ॥
NE 08 इं इच्छा सिद्धौ नमः ॥

NE to SW diagonal has two devatas each.
NE 09 पं प्राप्ति सिद्धौ नमः ॥
SW 10 सं सर्वकाम सिद्धौ नमः ॥

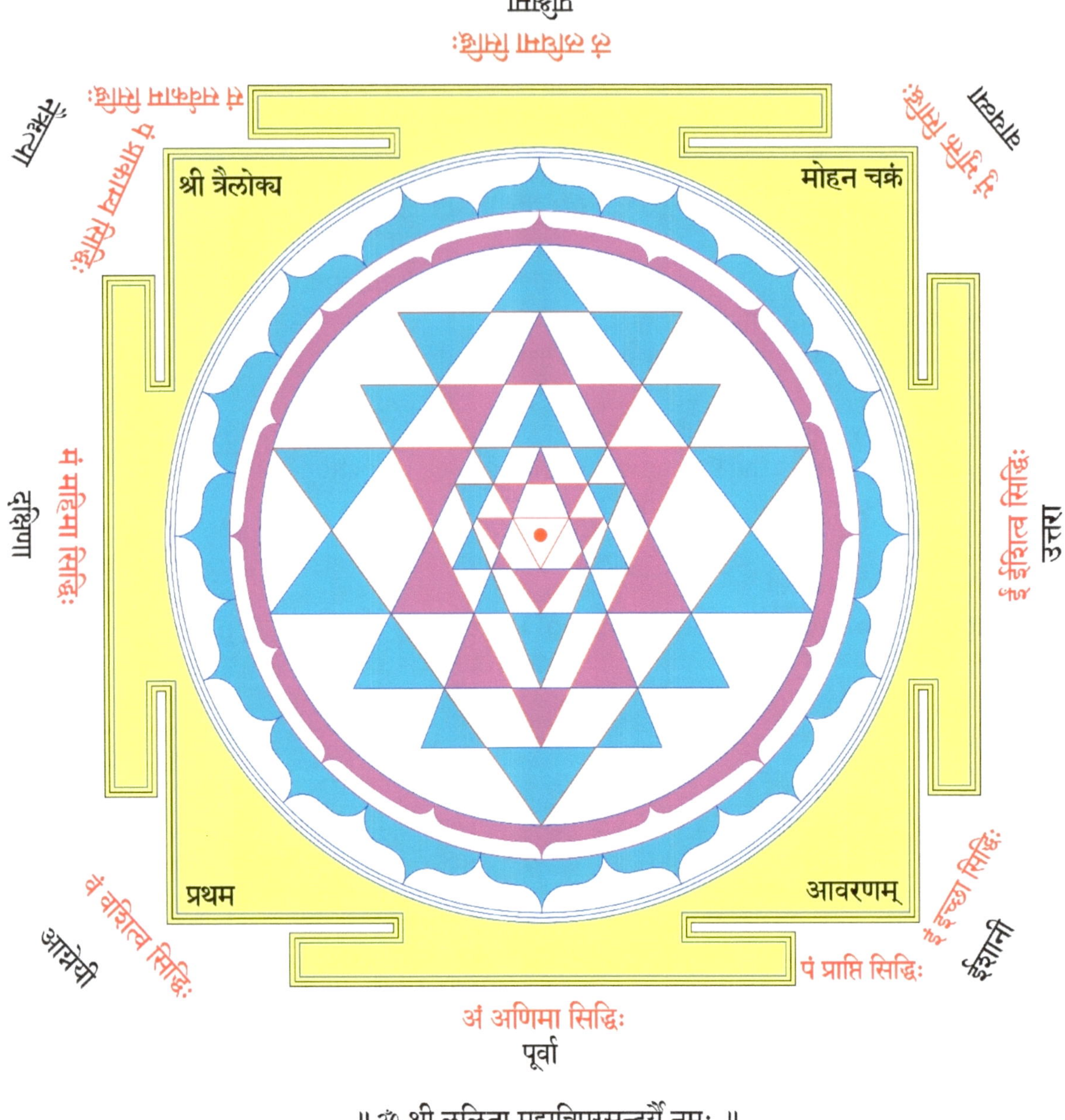

॥ ॐ श्री ललिता महात्रिपुरसुन्दर्यै नमः ॥

श्री यन्त्रम्

1st Enclosure –Four Sided Gates = भूपुर Bhūpura श्री त्रैलोक्यमोहन चक्रं प्रथमावरणम्

1st Enclosure Inscription View

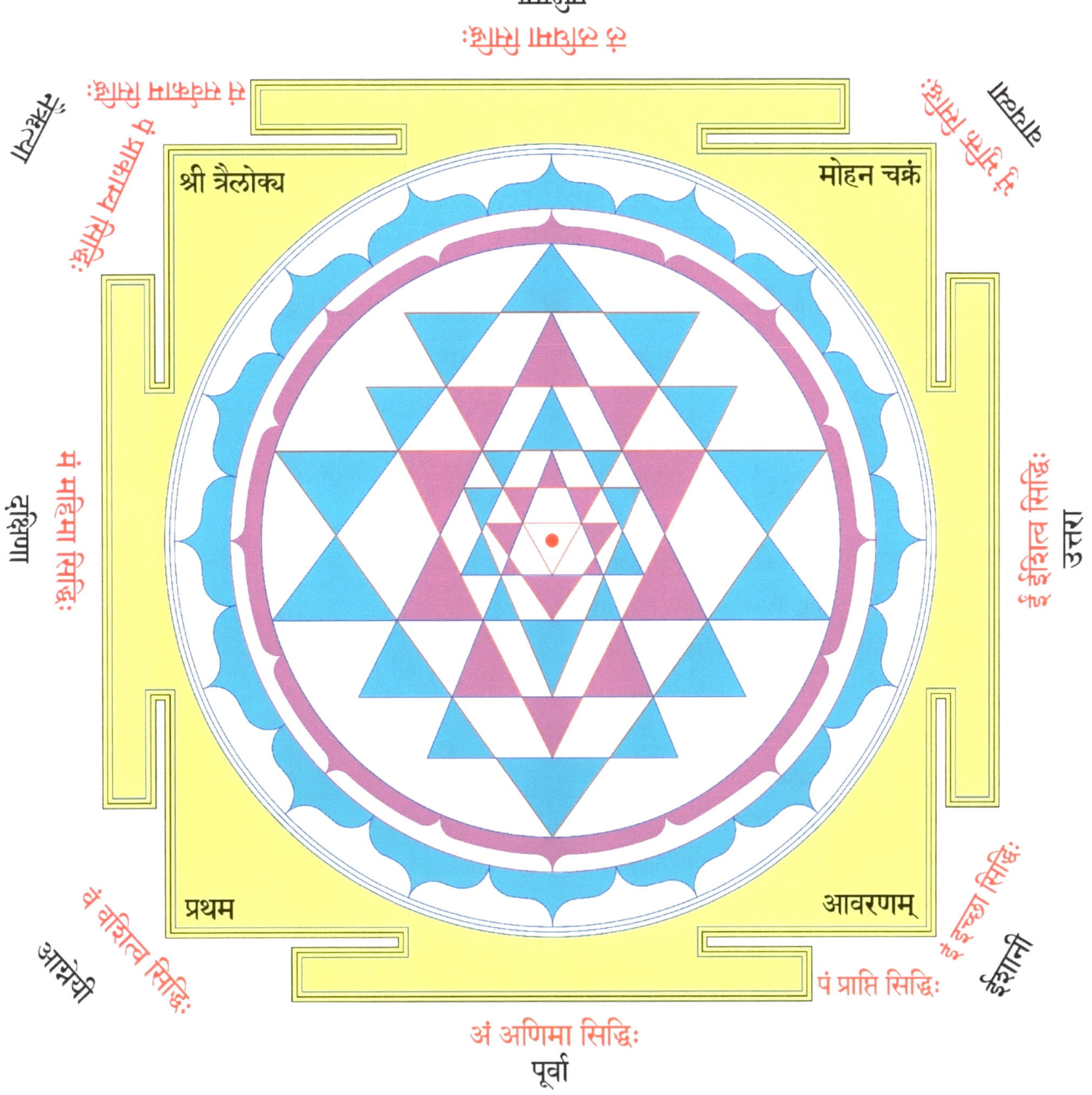

Move Clockwise, starting from अं bottom tip (East). Cover the 4 Cardinal Directions E S W N.

Now move Clockwise, starting from वं bottom left tip (South East). Ordinal Directions SE SW NW NE.

1. East अं अणिमासिद्धिः 2. South मं महिमासिद्धिः 3. West लं लघिमासिद्धिः 4. North ई ईशित्वसिद्धिः

5. SouthEast वं वशित्वसिद्धिः 6. SouthWest पं प्राकाम्यसिद्धिः 7. NorthWest भुं भुक्तिसिद्धिः 8. NorthEast इं इच्छासिद्धिः

<u>NE to SW diagonal has two divinities each.</u>

9. NE पं प्राप्तिसिद्धिः 10. SW सं सर्वकामसिद्धिः

2nd Enclosure Dvitīyā Āvaraṇa – Sixteen Flower Petals

पृथिवी-अप-तेजः-वायु-आकाश-श्रोत्र-त्वक्-चक्षुः-जिह्वा-घ्राण-वाक्-पाणि-पाद-पायु-उपस्थ-मनोविकाराः कामाकर्षिणी आदि षोडश शक्तयः ॥ १३ ॥

pṛthivī-apa-tejaḥ-vāyu-ākāśa-śrotra-tvak-cakṣuḥ-jihvā-ghrāṇa-vāk-pāṇi-pāda-pāyu-upastha-manovikārāḥ kāmākarṣiṇī ādi ṣoḍaśa śaktayaḥ ॥ 13 ॥

The elements Earth, Water, Fire, Air, Space; their sense attributes in reverse order - ears, skin, eyes, tongue, nose; and the organs of action Tongue, Hands, Feet, Anus, Penis; and the modifications of the mind; these are the sixteen divinities named Kamakarshini etc., stationed at this perimeter.

dvitīyāvaraṇa द्वितीयावरण = द्वितीय-आवरणम् sarvāśā paripūraka cakra श्री सर्व आशा परिपूरक चक्रं

16 petals - we go anticlockwise this time beginning from East (bottom).

Each petal has a vowel and the name of a goddess.

1. अं कामाकर्षिणी नित्यकलादेवी Kāmākarṣiṇī nityakalādevī

2. आं बुद्ध्यकर्षिणी नित्यकलादेवी Buddhyakarṣiṇī nityakalādevī

3. इं अहंकाराकर्षिणी नित्यकलादेवी Ahaṁkārākarṣiṇī nityakalādevī

4. ई शब्दाकर्षिणी नित्यकलादेवी Śabdākarṣiṇī nityakalādevī

5. उं स्पर्शाकर्षिणी नित्यकलादेवी Sparśākarṣiṇī nityakalādevī

6. ऊं रूपाकर्षिणी नित्यकलादेवी Rūpākarṣiṇī nityakalādevī

7. ऋं रसाकर्षिणी नित्यकलादेवी Rasākarṣiṇī nityakalādevī

8. ॠं गन्धाकर्षिणी नित्यकलादेवी Gandhākarṣiṇī nityakalādevī

9. लं चित्ताकर्षिणी नित्यकलादेवी Cittākarṣiṇī nityakalādevī

10. लृं धैर्याकर्षिणी नित्यकलादेवी Dhairyākarṣiṇī nityakalādevī

11. एं स्मृत्याकर्षिणी नित्यकलादेवी Smṛtyāākarṣiṇī nityakalādevī

12. ऐं नामाकर्षिणी नित्यकलादेवी Nāmākarṣiṇī nityakalādevī

13. ओं बीजाकर्षिणी नित्यकलादेवी Bījākarṣiṇī nityakalādevī

14. औं आत्माकर्षिणी नित्यकलादेवी Ātmākarṣiṇī nityakalādevī

15. अं अमृताकर्षिणी नित्यकलादेवी Amṛtākarṣiṇī nityakalādevī

16. अः शरीराकर्षिणी नित्यकलादेवी Śarīrākarṣiṇī nityakalādevī

अं कामाकर्षिण्यै नमः ॥ आं बुद्ध्याकर्षिण्यै नमः ॥ इं अहंकाराकर्षिण्यै नमः ॥ ई शब्दाकर्षिण्यै नमः ॥

उं स्पर्शाकर्षिण्यै नमः ॥ ऊं रूपाकर्षिण्यै नमः ॥ ऋं रसाकर्षिण्यै नमः ॥ ॠं गन्धाकर्षिण्यै नमः ॥ लं चित्ताकर्षिण्यै नमः ॥

लृं धैर्याकर्षिण्यै नमः ॥

एं स्मृत्याकर्षिण्यै नमः ॥ ऐं नामाकर्षिण्यै नमः ॥ ओं बीजाकर्षिण्यै नमः ॥ औं आत्माकर्षिण्यै नमः ॥

अं अमृताकर्षिण्यै नमः ॥ अः शरीराकर्षिण्यै नमः ॥

Sri Yantra

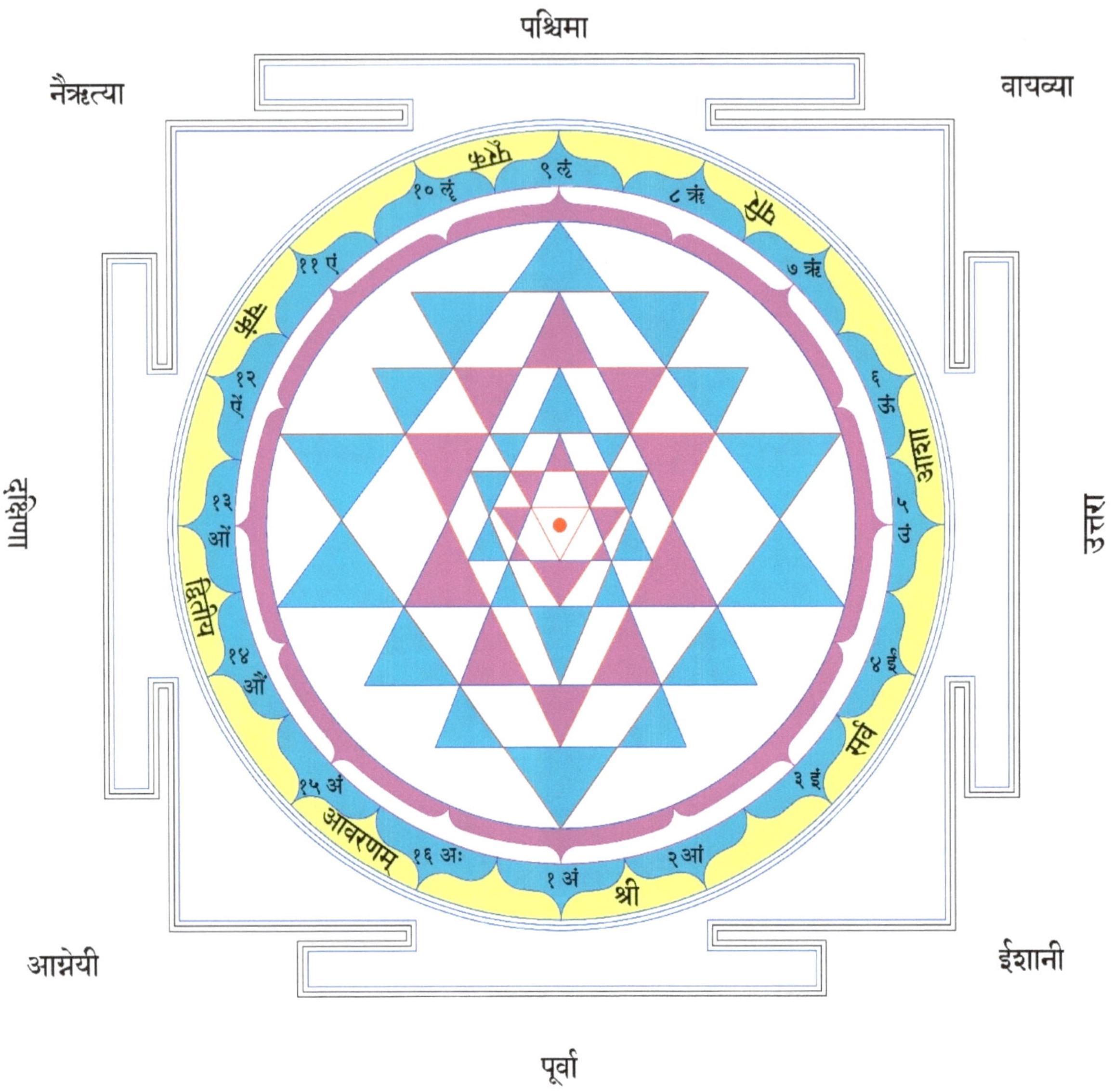

2nd Enclosure –Sixteen Petalled Lotus = षोडशदल पद्म Ṣoḍaśadala Padma श्री सर्वाशा परिपूरक चक्रं द्वितीयावरणम्

2nd Enclosure Inscription View

Move AntiClockwise, starting from अं bottom tip (East). Cover Sixteen Petals.

Notes:

अं = nazalised vowel

आं इं ईं उं ऊं ऋं ॠं ऌं ॡं एं ऐं ओं औं = in sequence the vowels of the Sanskrit Alphabet

Followed by the ayogavahas अं अः = till the end of the sixteen petals of the 2nd enclosure.

3rd Enclosure Tṛtīyā Āvaraṇa – Eight Flower Petals

वचन-आदान-गमन-विसर्ग-आनन्द-हान-उपादान-उपेक्षा-बुद्धयः अन्-अङ्ग-कुसुमा आदि शक्तयः अष्टौ ॥ १४ ॥

vacana-ādāna-gamana-visarga-ānanda-hāna-upādāna-upekṣā-buddhayaḥ an-aṅga-kusumā ādi śaktayaḥ aṣṭau ‖ 14 ‖

Soulful Speech, Acceptance of peoples and situations, Exploring far and beyond, Shedding unwanted stuff, Experiencing bliss, Sacrificing, Acquiring Wisdom, and Detachment, are the qualities of a mature and evolved intellect. These constitute the eight bodiless divinities named Kusuma etc.

tṛtīyāvaraṇam तृतीयावरणम् = तृतीय-आवरणम् sarva saṁkṣobhaṇa cakra श्री सर्व संक्षोभण चक्रं
8 petals - Clockwise starting from top petal (west) going alternative petals
each petal has a consonant group (starting letter) and the name of a goddess

Move Clockwise, starting from कं top tip (West). Cover the 4 Cardinal Directions W N E S.

1. West कं खं गं घं ङं अनङ्ग कुसुमा देवी anaṅga kusumā devī

2. North चं छं जं झं ञं अनङ्ग मेखला देवी anaṅga mekhalā devī

3. East टं ठं डं ढं णं अनङ्ग मदना देवी anaṅga madanā devī

4. South तं थं दं धं नं अनंग मदनातुरा देवी anaṅga madanāturā devī

Now move Clockwise, starting from पं top right tip (North West). Ordinal Directions NW NE SE SW.

5. NorthWest पं फं बं भं मं अनङ्ग रेखा देवी anaṅga rekhā devī

6. NorthEast यं रं लं वं अनङ्ग वेगिनी देवी anaṅga veginī devī

7. SouthEast शं षं सं हं अनङ्ग अङ्कुशा देवी anaṅga aṅkuśā devī

8. SouthWest ळं क्षं अनङ्ग मालिनी देवी anaṅga mālinī devī

॥ ॐ श्री ललिता महात्रिपुरसुन्दर्यै नमः ॥

श्री यन्त्रम्

3rd Enclosure –Eight Petalled Lotus = अष्टदल पद्म Aṣṭadala Padma श्री सर्व सौभाग्यदायक चक्रं तृतीयावरणम्

Move Clockwise, starting from कं top tip (West). Cover the 4 Cardinal Directions W N E S.

1. West कं खं गं घं ङं 2. North चं छं जं झं जं 3. East टं ठं डं ढं णं 4. South तं थं दं धं नं

Now move Clockwise, starting from पं top right tip (North West). Ordinal Directions NW NE SE SW.

5. NorthWest पं फं बं भं मं 6. NorthEast यं रं लं वं 7. SouthEast शं षं सं हं 8. SouthWest ळं क्षं

Magic of Numbers vis-a-vis the Triangle

Various scriptures describe the **human mind body** complex using different numbers.

The Bhagavad Gita uses the numbers 10, 8 in different verses.
Here in the Sri Yantra, we see there are 10 Outer Triangles of the fifth Enclosure.
Also, there are 10 Inner Triangles of the sixth Enclosure.
And, there are 8 Triangles of the seventh Enclosure.

The Vijnana Bhairava by Swami Lakshman Joo in its commentary of the 54th verse points to 36 elements
in creation. Guruji also said this during Maha Shivaratri 2016 at Bangalore Ashram.
If we consider the different aspects of the Sri Yantra, we can discriminate as:
1st Enclosure = 4 Outer Gates = represents the cardinal directions
2nd Enclosure = 16 Outer Petals = represents all vowels
3rd Enclosure = 8 Inner Petals = represents all consonants
7th Enclosure = 8 Triangles = represents the entire Sanskrit Alphabet, all sounds in speech
Sum = 4+16+8+8 = 36 represents all 36 elements (principle or *tattva*) in creation.

The Mandukya Upanishad says that 19 facets can be culled on the physical plane:
i. Bones, ii. Muscles, iii. Nerves, iv. Organs, v. Fluids, vi. five breaths, xi. five senses, xvi. Mind,
xvii. Intellect, xviii. Ego, xix. Citta (memory), xx. SELF = 20 aspects in living creation.
Here, 20 – 1 (the SELF) = 19 physical assets.

A Centered Triangular Number given by $(3n^2+3n+2)/2$ results in 19 for $n = 3$.

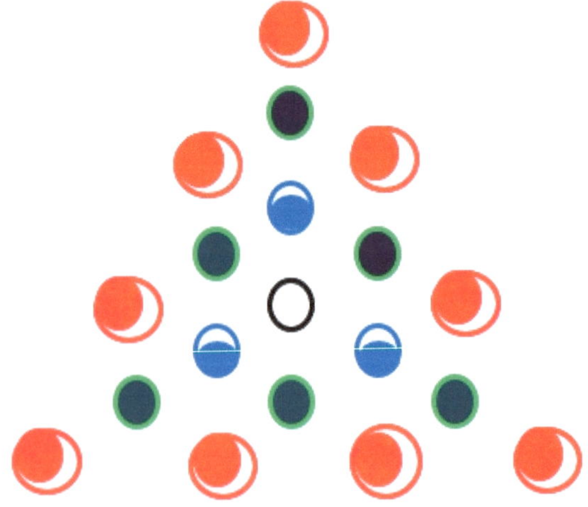

The Sri Yantra consists of many isosceles Triangles.

4th Enclosure Turiyā Āvaraṇa – Fourteen Triangles

अलम्बुषा कुहूः विश्वोदरा वारणा हस्तिजिह्वा यशोवती पयस्विनी गान्धारी पूषा शङ्खिनी सरस्वती इडा पिङ्गला सुषुम्ना चेति चतुर्दशः नाड्यः । सर्व-संक्षोभिणी आदि चतुर्दशारगा देवताः ॥ १५ ॥

alambuṣā kuhūḥ viśvodarā vāraṇā hastijihvā yaśovatī payasvinī gāndhārī pūṣā śaṅkhinī sarasvatī iḍā piṅgalā suṣumnā ceti caturdaśaḥ nāḍyaḥ | sarva-saṃkṣobhiṇī ādi caturdaśāragā devatāḥ ॥ 15 ॥

Alambusha, Kuhu, Vishvodara, Hastijihva, Yashovati, Payasvini, Gandhari, Pusha, Sankhini, Saraswati, ida, Pingala, and Sushumna are the fourteen subtle channels nadi. Their corresponding divinities named Sarvasankshobhini, etc. rule the fourteen triangles.

turiyāvaraṇa (fourth enclosure) तुरियावरणम् sarva-saubhāgya-dāyaka cakra श्री सर्व सौभाग्य-दायक चक्रं fourteen outer triangles - we go anticlockwise this time beginning from East (bottom) R.Rao

with consonants in each triangle beginning with क.

कं सर्वसंक्षोभिणी शक्ति East 1. Sarvasaṃkṣobhiṇī śakti

खं सर्वविद्रविणी शक्ति 2.Sarvavidraviṇī śakti

गं सर्वाकर्षिणि शक्ति 3. Sarvākarṣiṇi

घं सर्वाह्लादिनी शक्ति 4. Sarvāhlādinī

ङं सर्वसंमोहिनी शक्ति 5. Sarvasaṁmohinī

चं सर्वस्तंभिनी शक्ति 6. Sarvastaṁbhinī

छं सर्वजृंभिणी शक्ति 7. Sarvajṛṁbhiṇī

जं सर्ववशङ्करी शक्ति 8. Sarvavaśaṅkarī

झं सर्वरञ्जनी शक्ति 9. Sarvarañjanī

ञं सर्वोन्मादिनी शक्ति 10. Sarvonmādinī

टं सर्वार्थसाधिनी शक्ति 11. Sarvārthasādhinī

ठं सर्वसंपत्तिपूरणी शक्ति 12. Sarvasaṁpattipūraṇī

डं सर्वमन्त्रमयी शक्ति 13. Sarvamantramayī

ढं सर्वद्वन्द्वक्षयङ्करी शक्ति 14. Sarvadvandvakṣayaṅkarī śakti

कं सर्व संक्षोभिण्यै नमः ॥   खं सर्व विद्राविण्यै नमः ॥   गं सर्व आकर्षिण्यै नमः ॥   घं सर्वा ह्लादिन्यै नमः ॥   ङं सर्व संमोहिन्यै नमः ॥

चं सर्व स्तंभिन्यै नमः ॥   छं सर्व जृंभिन्यै नमः ॥   जं सर्व वशंकर्यै नमः ॥   झं सर्व रंजन्यै नमः ॥   ञं सर्वोन्मादिन्यै नमः ॥

टं सर्वाथ साधिन्यै नमः ॥   ठं सर्व संपत्ति पूरिण्यै नमः ॥   डं सर्व मंत्रमय्यै नमः ॥   ढं सर्व द्वंद्वक्षयं कर्यै नमः ॥

यः एवं वेद , आत्मना आत्मानं एव संविशति the one who so understands, by the Self into the Self alone he merges.

Sri Yantra

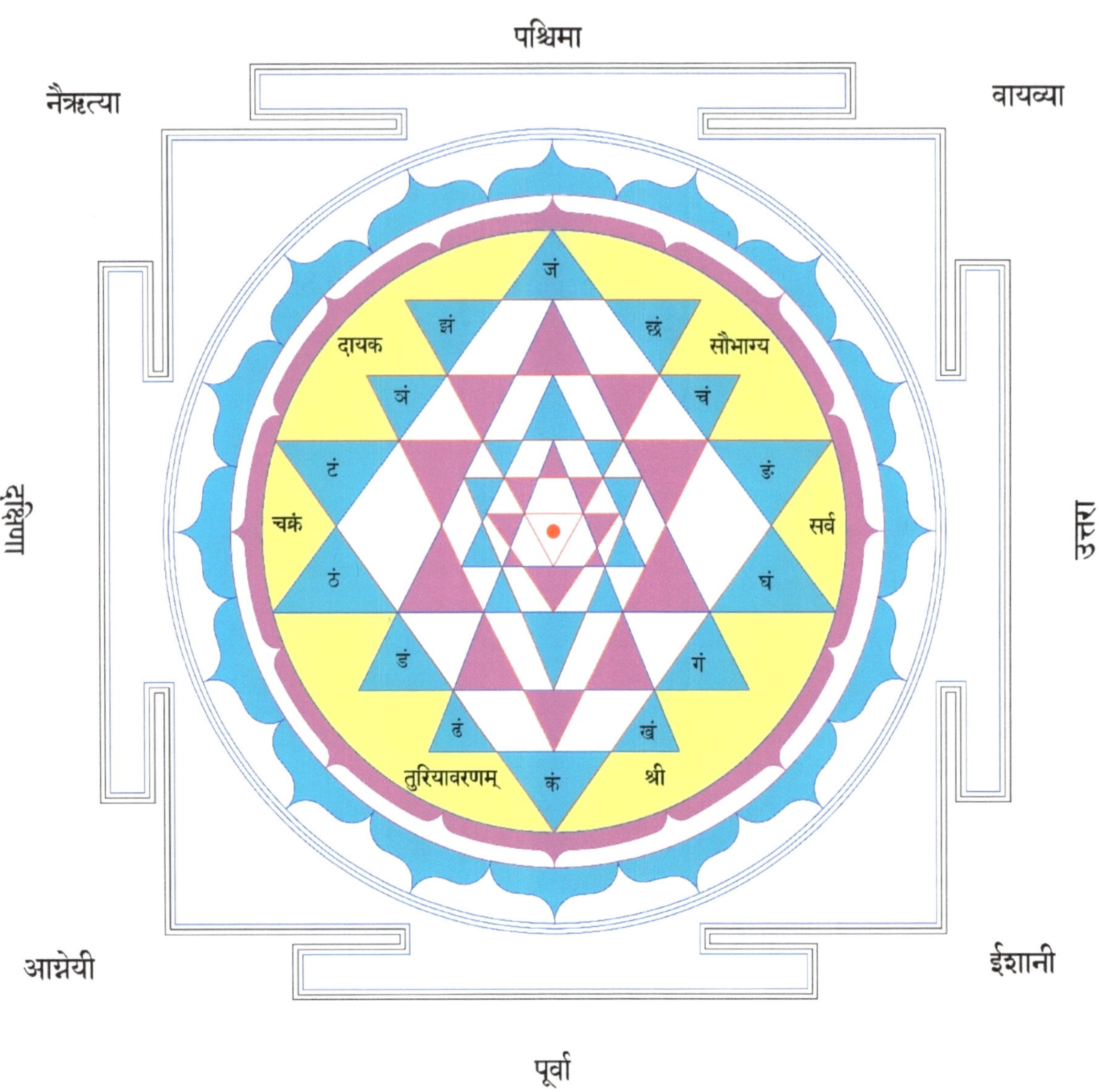

4th Enclosure –Fourteen Triangles = चतुर्दशार Caturdaśāra श्री सर्व सौभाग्यदायक चक्रं तुरियावरणम्
(In spiritual texts, the **fourth** state is called the **Turiya**).

Move AntiClockwise, starting from कं bottom tip (East). Cover Fourteen Triangles.

Notes:

कं = nazalised consonant begins, the Sanskrit Alphabet in continuation from 3rd enclosure

खं गं घं ङं चं छं जं झं ञं टं ठं डं ढं = till the end of the fourteen triangles of the 4th enclosure.

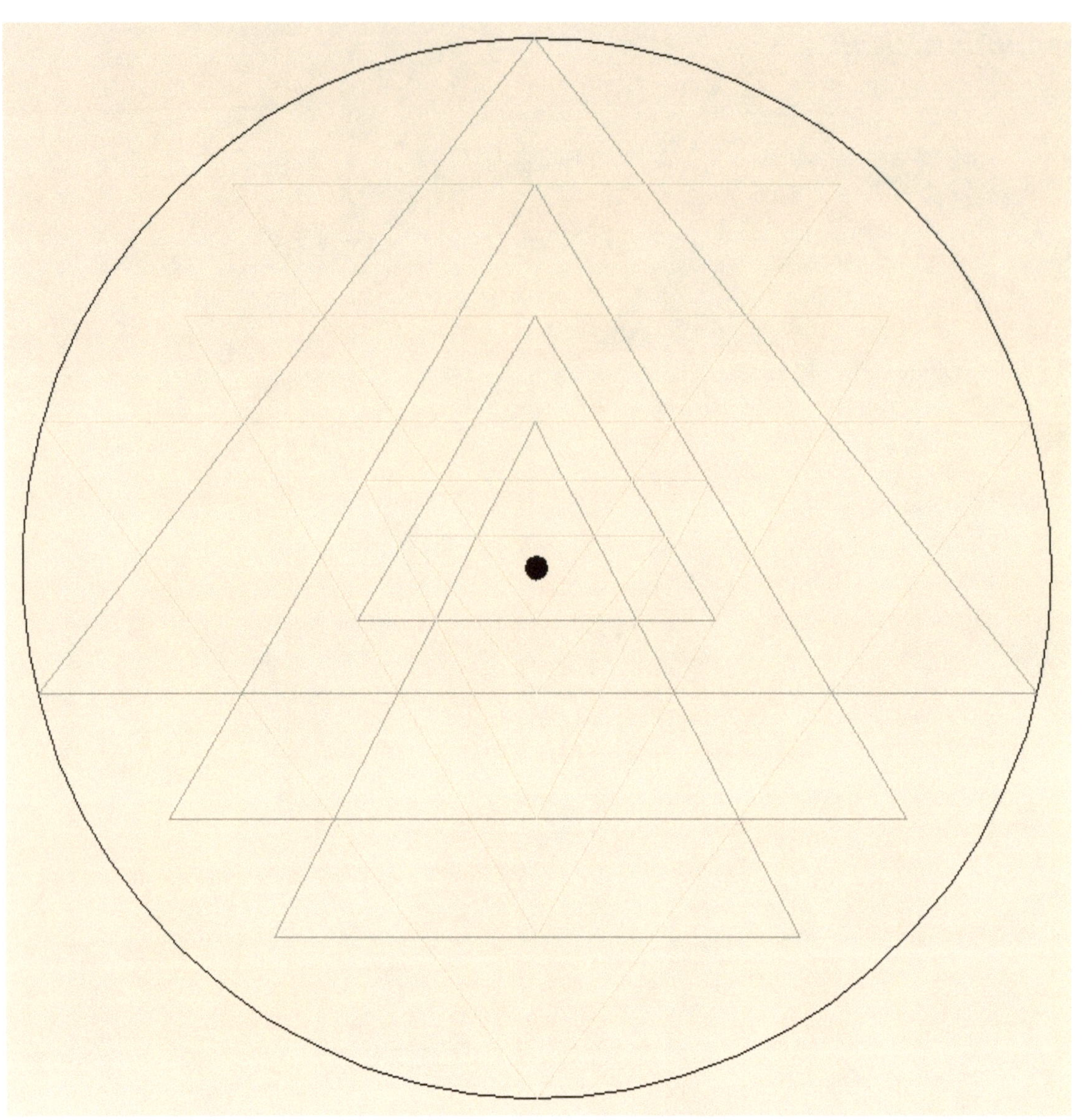

5th Enclosure Pañcamā Āvaraṇa – Ten Outer Triangles

प्राण-अपान-व्यान-उदान-समान-नाग-कूर्म-कृकर-देवदत्त-धनञ्जयाः इति दश वायवः । सर्व-सिद्धिप्रदा देव्यो बहिर्दशारगा देवताः ॥ १६

prāṇa-apāna-vyāna-udāna-samāna-nāga-kūrma-kṛkara-devadatta-dhanañjayāḥ iti daśa vāyavaḥ | sarva-siddhipradā devyo bahirdaśāragā devatāḥ ॥ 16

The vital airs named
- Prana, Apana, Vyana, Udana, Samana;
- Naga, Kurma, Krikara, Devadutta, Dhananjaya

constitute the divinites guarding the ten outer triangles.

fifth āvaraṇa pañcamāvaraṇa पञ्चमावरणम् Sarvārthasādhakacakra श्री सर्व अर्थ-साधक चक्रं

Ten triangles - we go anticlockwise this time beginning from East (bottom).

With consonants in each triangle in continuation from above.

णं सर्वसिद्धिप्रदा देवी East 1. Sarvasiddhipradā devī

तं सर्वसंपत्प्रदा देवी 2. Sarvasaṁpatpradā devī

थं सर्वप्रियङ्करी देवी 3. Sarvapriyaṅkarī devī

दं सर्वमङ्गलकारिणी देवी 4. Sarvamaṅgalakāriṇī devī

धं सर्वकामप्रदा देवी 5. Sarvakāmapradā devī

नं सर्वदुःखविमोचिनी देवी 6. Sarvaduḥkhavimocinī devī

पं सर्वमृत्युप्रशमनी देवी 7. Sarvamṛtyupraśamanī devī

फं सर्विघ्ननिवारिणी देवी 8. sarvighnanivāriṇī devī

बं सर्वाङ्गसुन्दरी देवी 9. Sarvāṅgasundarī devī

भं सर्वसौभाग्यदायिनी देवी 10. Sarvasaubhāgyadāyinī devī

णं सर्वसिद्धि प्रदायै नमः ॥

तं सर्व संपत् प्रदायै नमः॥ थं सर्व प्रियंकयैं नमः॥ दं सर्व मंगल कारिण्यै नमः॥ धं सर्व कामप्रदायै नमः॥

नं सर्व दुःख विमोचिन्यै नमः॥

पं सर्व मृत्यु प्रशमन्यै नमः ॥ फं सर्व विघ्न निवारिण्यै नमः ॥ बं सर्वांग सुंदर्यैं नमः ॥ भं सर्व सौभाग्य दायियन्यै नमः ॥

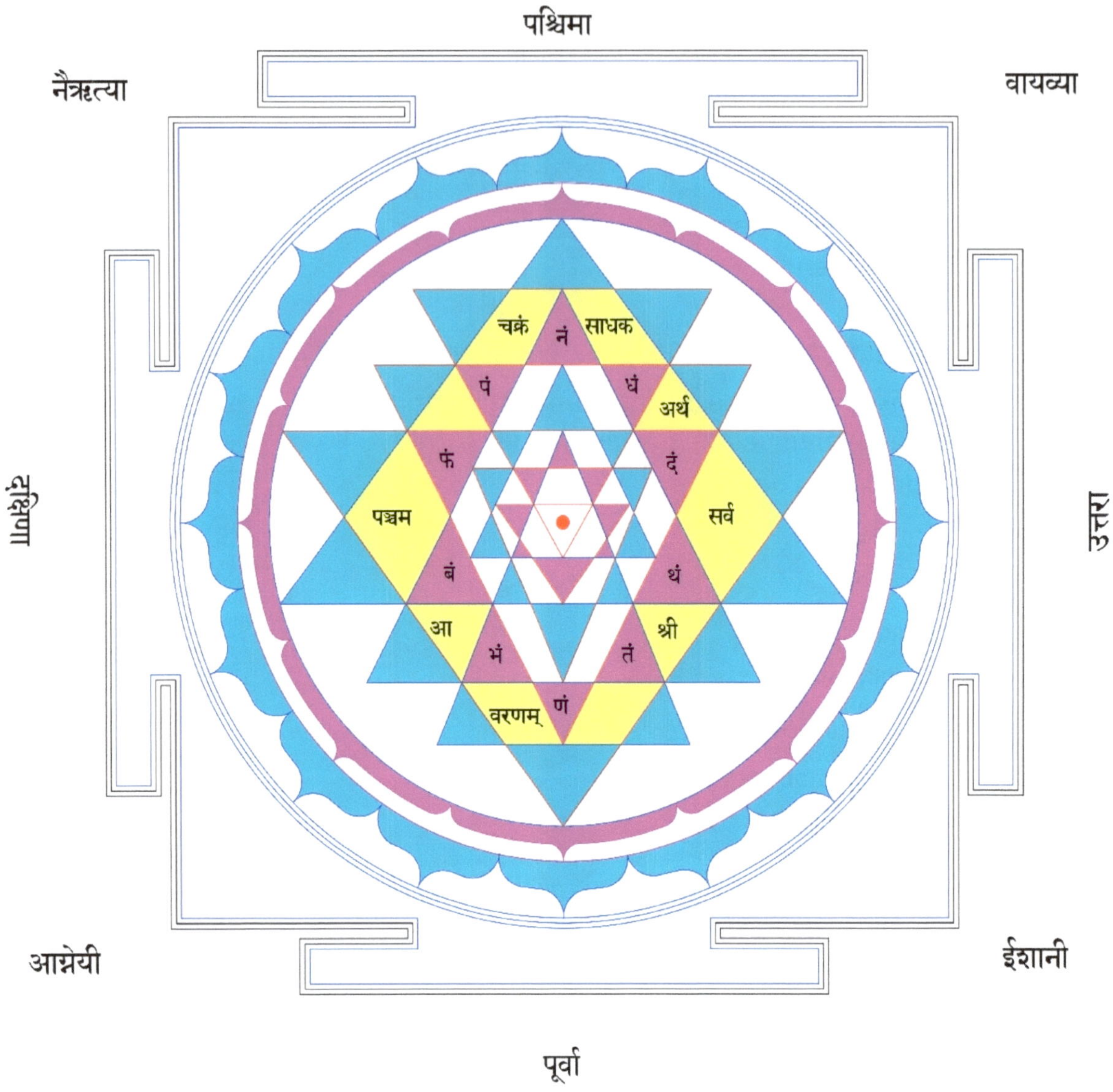

5th Enclosure – Outer Ten Triangles = बहिर्दशार BahirDaśāra श्री सर्वार्थसाधक चक्रं पञ्चमावरणम्

5th Enclosure Inscription View

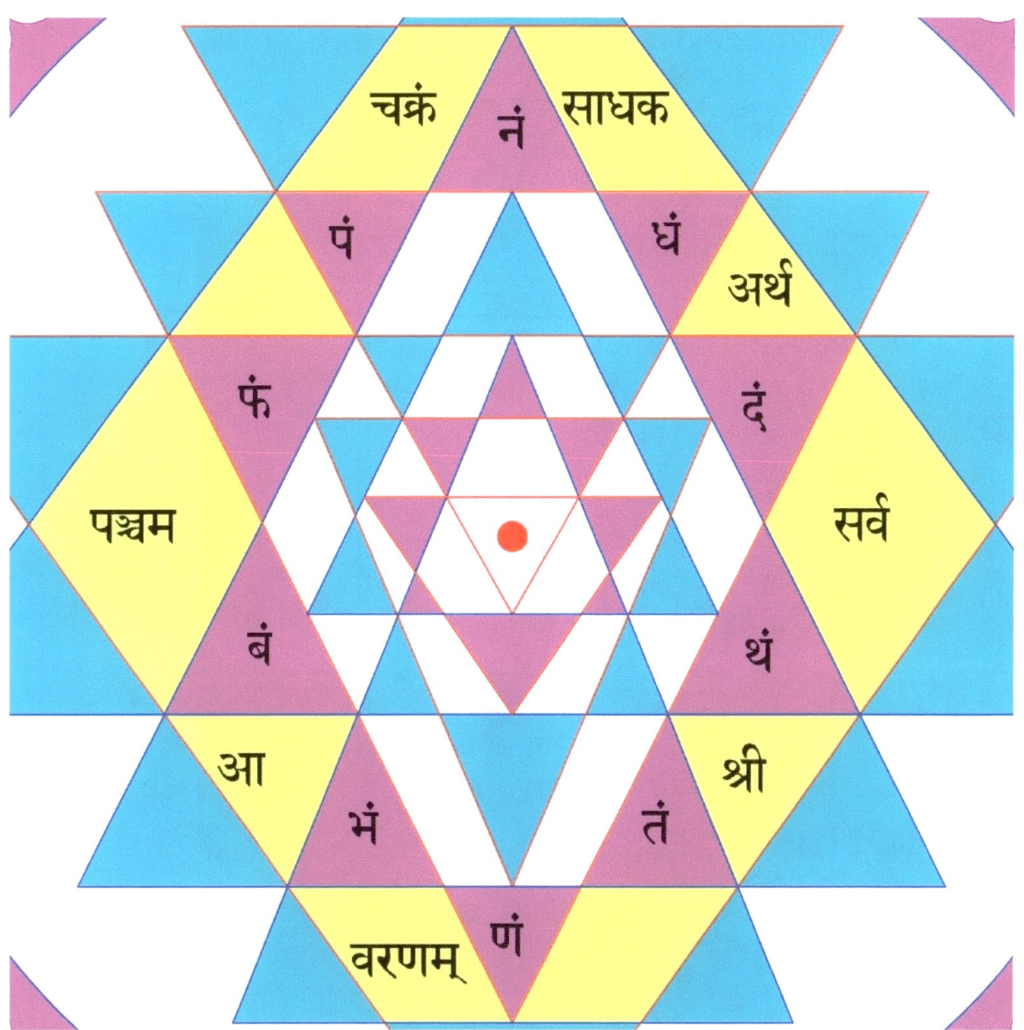

Move AntiClockwise, starting from णं bottom tip (East). Cover Ten Triangles.

Notes:

णं = nazalised consonant in continuation from 4th enclosure

तं थं दं धं नं पं फं बं भं = till the end of the ten triangles of the 5th enclosure.

6th Enclosure Ṣaṣṭhā Āvaraṇa – Ten Inner Triangles

एतद् वायु-दशक संसर्गोपाधिभेधेन रेचक-पाचक-शोषक-दाहक-प्लावकाःअमृतम् इति प्राणमुख्यत्वेन पञ्चधा जठर-अग्निः भवति ॥ १७॥

क्षारकः उद्वारकः क्षोभकः मोहकः जृम्भकः इति नाग-प्राधान्येन पञ्चविधोऽस्ति । तेन मनुष्याणां देहानां भक्ष्य-भोज्य-चोष्य-लेह्य-पेयात्मकं पञ्चविधम्-अन्नं पाचयन्ति ॥ १८ ॥ एता दश वह्निकलाः सर्वज्ञाद्याः अन्तर्दशारगा देवताः ॥ १९ ॥

etad vāyu-daśaka saṃsargopādhibhedhena recaka-pacaka-śoṣaka-dāhaka-plāvakāḥamṛtam iti

prāṇamukhyatvena pañcadhā jaṭhara-agniḥ bhavati ‖ 17‖   kṣārakaḥ udgārakaḥ kṣobhakaḥ mohakaḥ

jṛmbhakaḥ iti nāga-prādhānyena pañcavidho'sti | tena manuṣyāṇāṃ mohako dāhako bhakṣya-bhojya-

coṣya-lehya-peyātmakaṃ pañcavidham-annaṃ pācayanti ‖ 18 ‖ etā daśa vahnikalāḥ sarvajñādyāḥ

antardaśāragā devatāḥ ‖ 19 ‖

As per the prevailing situation and demand, the same ten-fold Prana:
functions as the five-fold **main** Prana as
- The Remover of toxins
- The Digester of good emotions, thoughts, and food
- The Smoother of slushy, nagging and sticky emotions
- The Vanquisher of painful memories
- The Submerger of traumatic thoughts, to stoke the digestive fires in the stomach and abdomen,

and led by the upaPrana named Naga functions as the five-fold **secondary** Prana as
- The Secreter
- The Ejector
- The Churner
- The Sweller
- The Yawner

These constitute the divinites guarding the ten inner triangles.

sixth āvaraṇa (ṣaṣṭhāvaraṇa) षष्ठावरणम् Sarvarakṣākaracakra श्री सर्व रक्षा-कर चक्रं

Ten triangles - we go anticlockwise this time beginning from East (bottom)
with consonants in each triangle in continuation from above.

मं सर्वज्ञादेवी East 1. Sarvajñādevī

यं सर्वशक्तिप्रदादेवी 2. Sarvaśaktidevī

रं सर्वैश्वर्यप्रदादेवी 3. Sarvaiśvaryapradādevī

लं सर्वज्ञानमयीदेवी 4. Sarvajñānamayīdevī

वं सर्वव्याधिविनाशिनीदेवी 5. Sarvavyādhivināśinīdevī

शं सर्वाधारादेवी 6. Sarvādhārādevī

षं सर्वपापहरादेवी 7. Sarvapāpaharādevī

सं सर्वानन्दमयीदेवी 8. Sarvānandamayīdevī

हं सर्वरक्षास्वरूपिणीदेवी 9. Sarvarakṣāsvarūpiṇīdevī

ळं क्षं सर्वेप्सितफलप्रदादेवी 10. Sarvepsitaphalapradādevī

मं सर्वज्ञायै नमः ॥ यं सर्व शक्तै नमः ॥ रं सर्वैश्वर्य प्रदायै नमः ॥ लं ज्ञानमय्यै नमः ॥ वं सर्व व्याधि विनाशिन्यै नमः ॥

शं सर्वाधार स्वरूपायै नमः ॥ षं सर्व पापहरायै नमः ॥ सं सर्वानन्दमयू नमः ॥ हं सर्व रक्षारूपिणीयै नमः ॥

ळं क्षं सर्वेप्सित फलप्रदायै नमः ॥

Sri Yantra

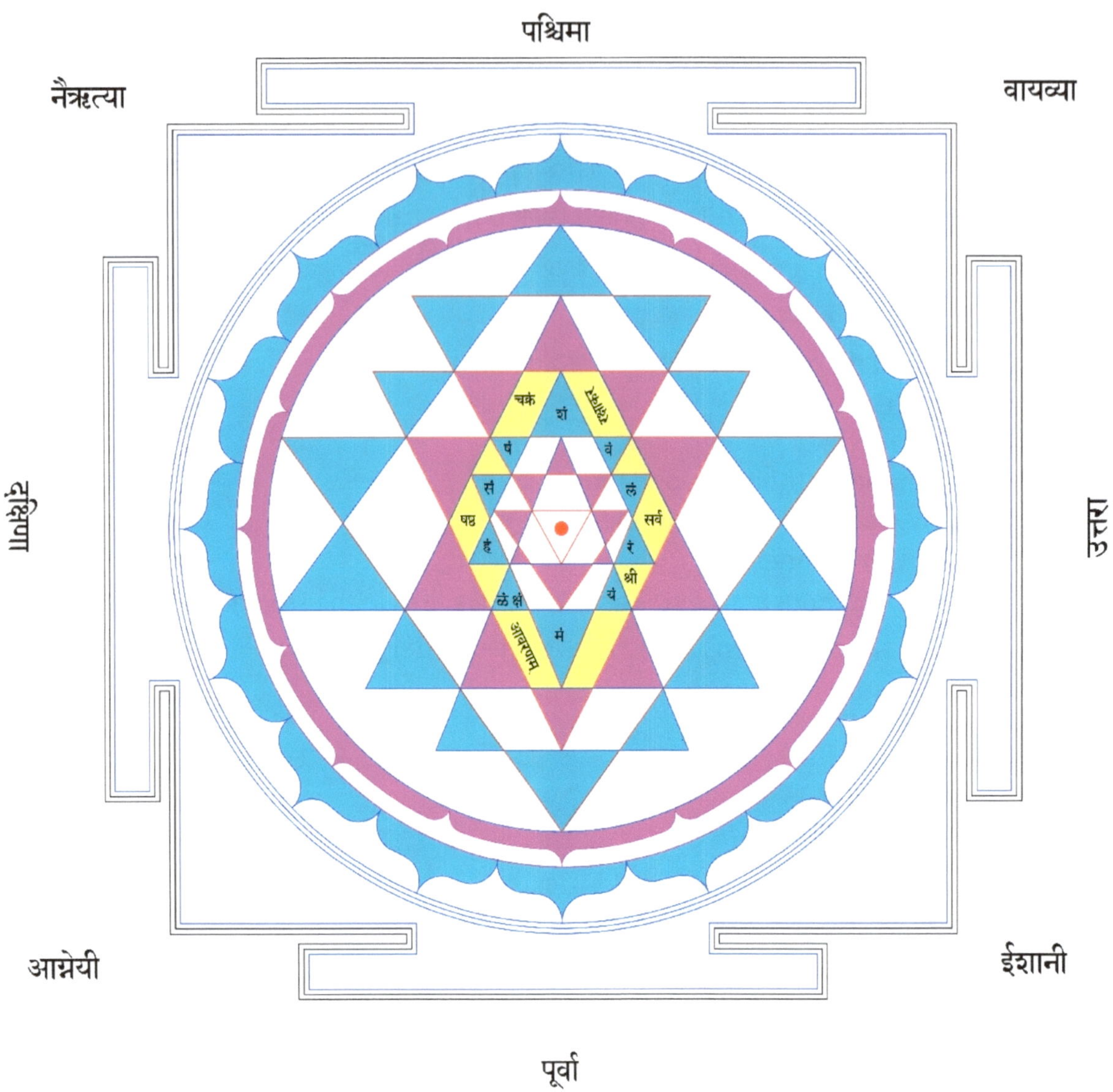

6th Enclosure – Inner Ten Triangles = अन्तर्दशार AntarDaśāra श्री सर्व रक्षाकर चक्रं षष्ठावरणम्

6th Enclosure Inscription View

Move AntiClockwise, starting from मं bottom tip (East). Cover Ten Triangles.

Notes:

मं = nazalised consonant in continuation from 5th enclosure

यं लं रं वं शं षं सं हं = till the end of the standard Sanskrit Alphabet

ळं क्षं = additional letters of the Vedic Sanskrit Alphabet

7th Enclosure Saptamā Āvaraṇa – Eight Triangles

शीत-उष्ण-सुख-दुःख-इच्छाः सत्त्व-रजस्-तमोगुणाः वशिनी आदि शक्तयः अष्टौ ॥ २० ॥

sīta-uṣṇa-sukha-duḥkha-icchāḥ sattva-rajas-tamoguṇāḥ vaśinī ādi śaktayaḥ aṣṭau ॥ 20 ॥

The Coolness that pacifies, The Heat that nourishes, The Joys that delight, The Hardships that strengthen, The Intentions that manifest; The Sincere Awareness that protects, The Call to Action that supports, and The desire to Let Go and Relax that keeps one fresh and alive for another day; these are the eight goddesses circumambulating this wall of the fortress. Named Vashini etc.

seventh āvaraṇa or saptamāvaraṇam सप्तमावरणम् sarvarogaharacakra श्री सर्व रोग-हर चक्रं

eight triangles – अष्टार Aṣṭāra

we go anticlockwise this time beginning from East (bottom) to write the entire sanskrit alphabet

अं आं इं ईं उं ऊं ऋं ॠं लं ॡं एं ऐं ओं औं अं अः वशिनी वाग्देवी East 1. Vaśinī vāgdevī

कं खं गं घं ङं कामेश्वरी वाग्देवी 2. Kāmeśvarī vāgdevī

चं छं जं झं जं मोदिनी वाग्देवी 3. Modinī vāgdevī

टं ठं डं ढं णं विमला वाग्देवी 4. Vimalā vāgdevī

तं थं दं धं नं अरुणा वाग्देवी 5. Aruṇā vāgdevī

पं फं बं भं मं जैनि वाग्देवी 6. Jaini vāgdevī

यं रं लं वं सर्वेश्वरी वाग्देवी 7. Sarveśvarī vāgdevī

शं षं सं हं ळं क्षं कौलिनी वाग्देवी 8. Kaulinī vāgdevī

1 East अं आं इं ईं उं ऊं ऋं ॠं लं ॡं एं ऐं ओं औं अं अः ब्ल्रूं वशिनी वाग्देवतायै नमः ॥

2 कं खं गं घं ङं क्ल्ह्रीं कामेश्वरी वाग्देवतायै नमः ॥ 3 चं छं जं झं जं न्ह्रीं मोदिनी वाग्देवतायै नमः ॥ 4 टं ठं डं ढं णं स्ल्रूं विमला वाग्देवतायै नमः ॥ 5 तं थं दं धं नं ज्म्रीं अरुणा वाग्देवतायै नमः ॥ 6 पं फं बं भं मं हृस्ल्व्यूं जयिनी वाग्देवतायै नमः ॥ 7 यं रं लं वं इ्झ्रयूं सर्वेश्वरी वाग्देवतायै नमः ॥ 8 शं षं सं हं ळं क्षं क्ष्म्रीं कौलिनी वाग्देवतायै नमः ॥

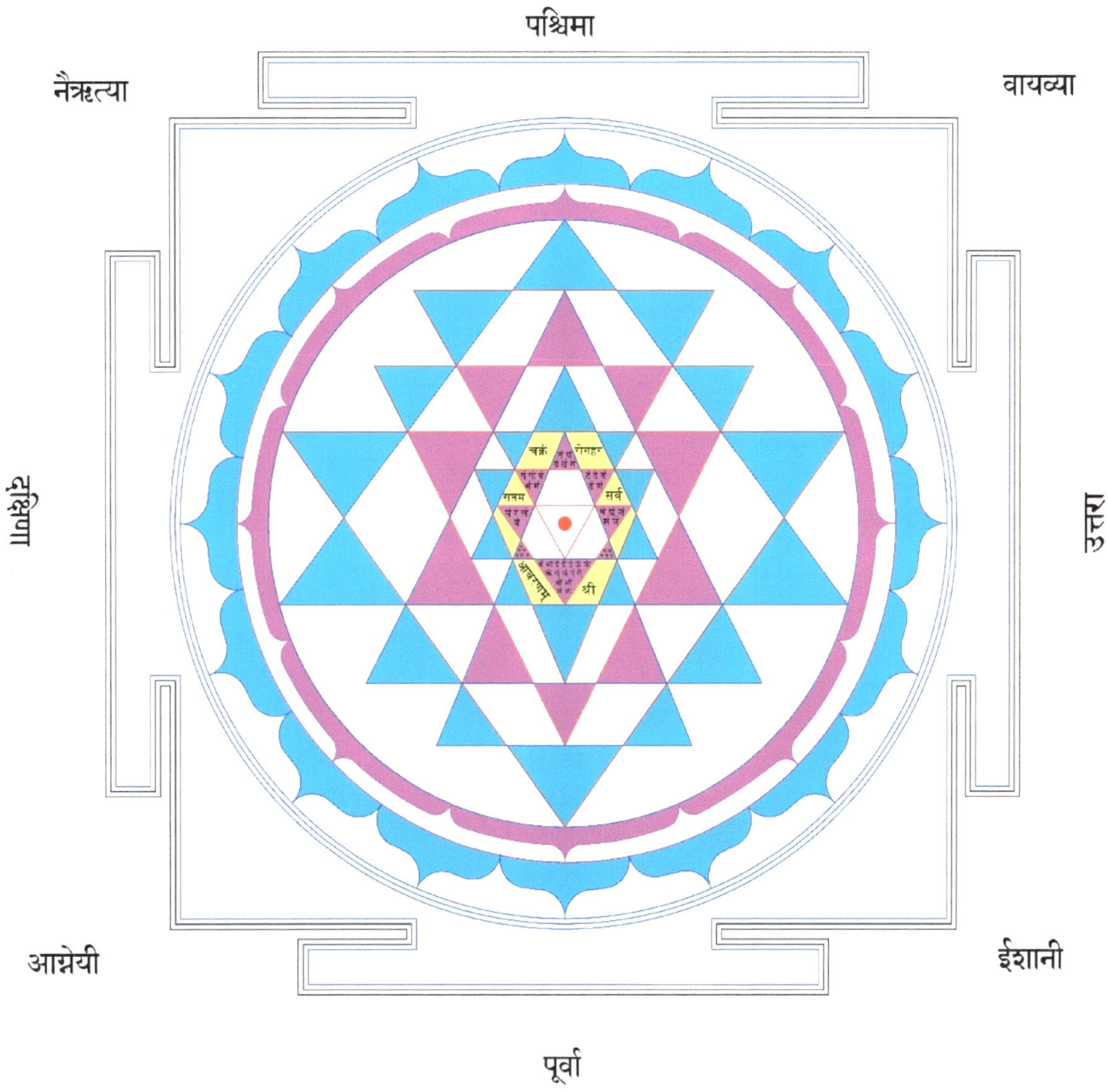

7th Enclosure - Eight Triangles = अष्टार Aṣṭāra श्री सर्व रोगहर चक्रं सप्तमावरणम्

Move AntiClockwise, starting from अच् bottom tip (East). Cover Eight Triangles. Called अष्टार Aṣṭāra.

Notes: Here we write the complete Sanskrit Alphabet, representing all the Speech Goddesses. From अं to क्षं

7th Enclosure Inscription View (Approximate)

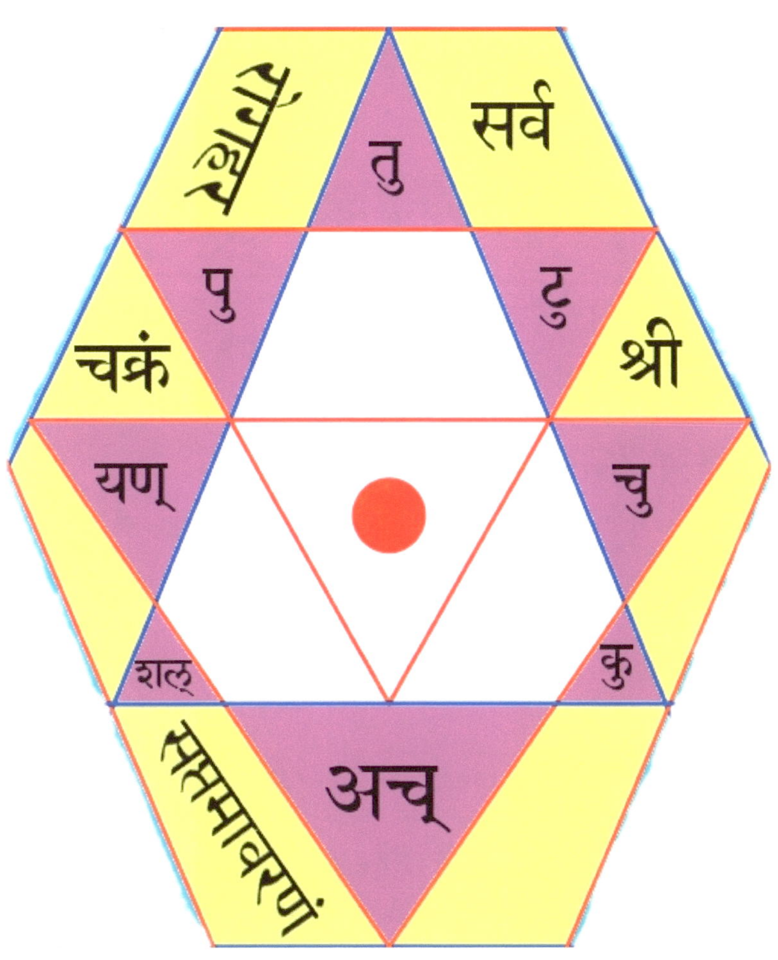

अच् pratyahara for all vowels, nazalised = अं आं इं ईं उं ऊं ऋं ॠं लं ॡं एं ऐं ओं औं , and ayogavahas अं अः

कुं = 1st row class consonants nazalised = कं खं गं घं ङं

चुं = 2nd row class consonants nazalised = चं छं जं झं ञं

टुं = 2nd row class consonants nazalised = टं ठं डं ढं णं

तुं = 2nd row class consonants nazalised = तं थं दं धं नं

पुं = 2nd row class consonants nazalised = पं फं बं भं मं

यण् = semivowels nazalised = यं लं रं वं

शल् pratyahara for sibilants, nazalised = शं षं सं हं , and extended alphabet ळं क्षं

8th Enclosure Aṣṭamā Āvaraṇa – Innermost Triangle

शब्द-स्पर्श-रूप-रस-गन्याः पञ्च-तन्मात्राः पञ्च-पुष्पबाणाः ॥ २१ ॥ मनः इक्षु-धनुः ॥ २२ ॥ रागः पाशः ॥ २३ ॥ द्वेषः अङ्कुशः ॥ २४ ॥

śabda-sparśa-rūpa-rasa-gandhāḥ pañca-tanmātrāḥ pañca-puṣpabāṇāḥ ॥ 21 ॥ manaḥ ikṣu-dhanuḥ ॥ 22 ॥

rāgaḥ pāśaḥ ॥ 23 ॥ dveṣaḥ aṅkuśaḥ ॥ 24 ॥

- Sound, Touch, Form, Taste, Smell are the five direct sensory tolerances, and are called the five alluring arrows.
- The thought producing Mind is the desirous bow ever shooting outwards
- The feeling of Infatuation is that which initially entangles and ultimately strangles
- The feeling of Aversion is that which hobbles and restricts one's own evolution.

अव्यक्त-महत्तत्त्वम्-महत्अहङ्काराः इति कामेश्वरी-वज्रेश्वरी-भगमालिनी अन्तस् त्रिकोण-अग्रगा देवताः ॥ २५ ॥

avyakta-mahattattvam-mahatahaṅkārāḥ iti kāmeśvarī-vajreśvarī-bhagamālinī antas trikoṇa-agragā devatāḥ ॥ 25 ॥

- The unmanifest primordial nature,
- The individual consciousness, and
- The human ego

are the leading divinities of this innermost triangle, also named Kameshwari, Vajreshwari, Bhagamalini.

Eighth āvaraṇa or aṣṭamāvaraṇam अष्टमावरणं called Sarvasiddhiprada श्री सर्व सिद्धि-प्रद चक्रं
one downward pointing triangle, white in color
we go clockwise this time beginning from East (bottom)

Tripurāmbācakreśvarī

East - Triangle Apex Down 1. ऐं
Triangle base left 2. क्लीं
Triangle base right 3. सौः

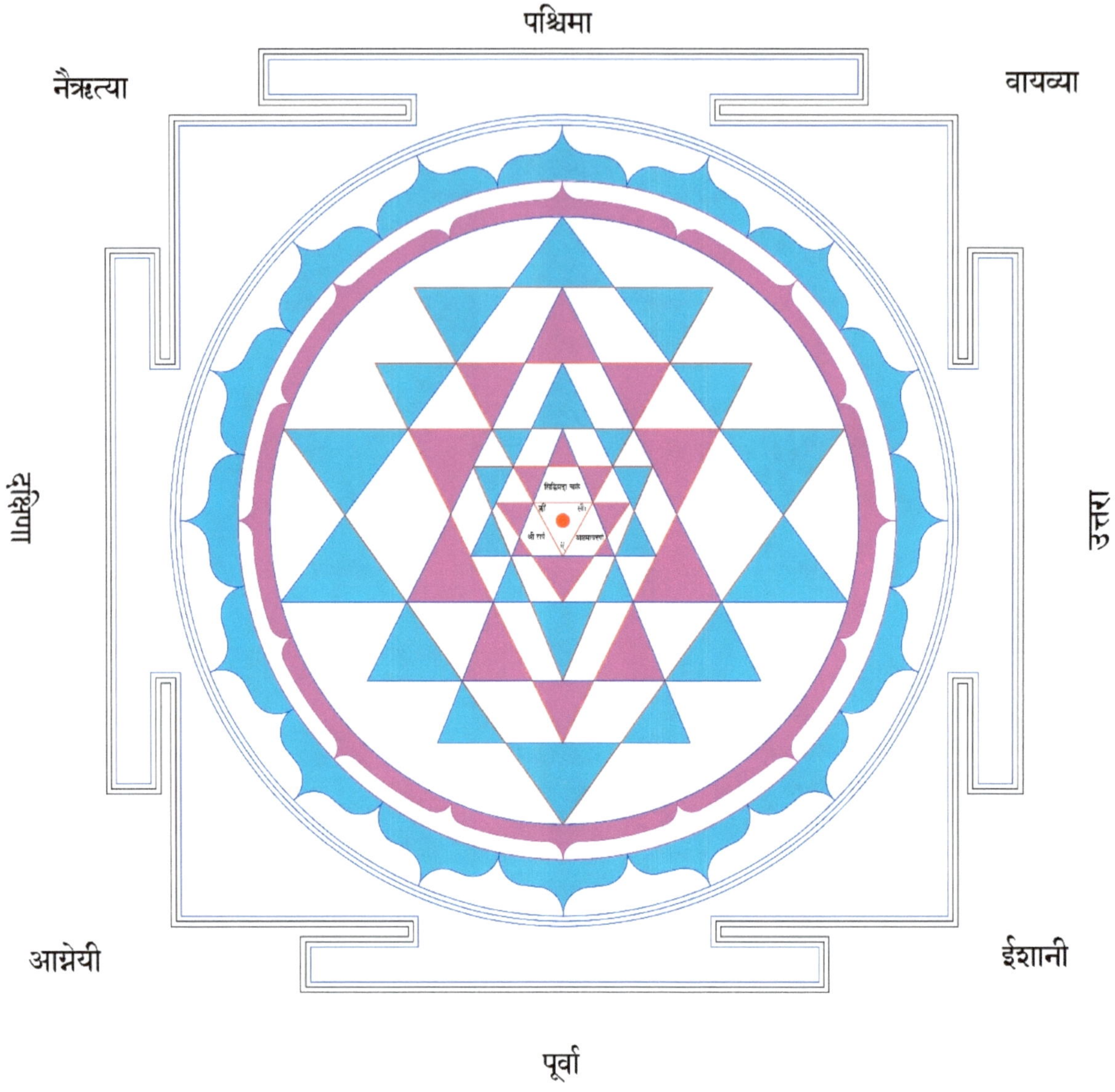

8th Enclosure – Innermost Triangle = त्रिकोण Trikoṇa श्री सर्व सिद्धिप्रद चक्रं अष्टमावरणम्

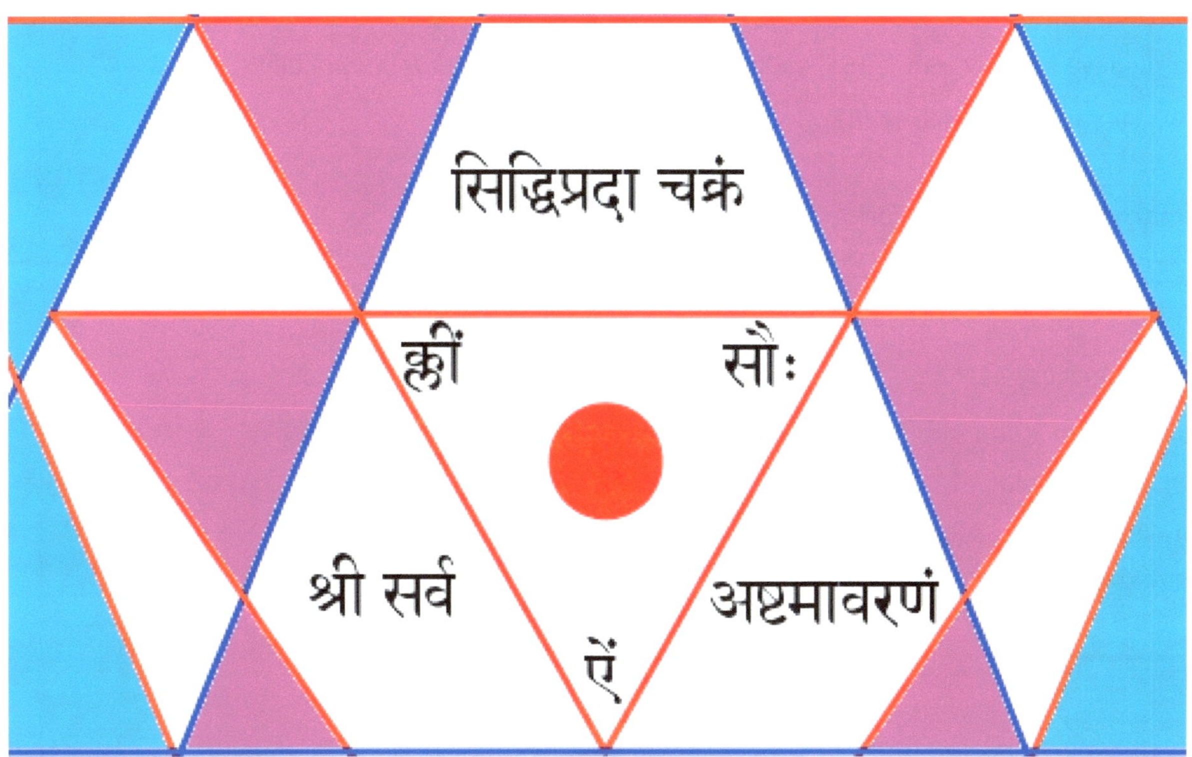

Move Clockwise, starting from एं bottom tip (East).

Notes: Here we write the symbols of Mother Divine

9th Enclosure Navamā Āvaraṇa - Bindu

निरुपाधिका संविदेव कामेश्वरः ॥ २६ ॥ सदानन्दपूर्णा स्वात्मैव परदेवता ललिता ॥ २७ ॥ लौहित्यमेतस्य सर्वस्य विमर्शः ॥ २८ ॥

nirupādhikā saṃvideva kāmeśvaraḥ ॥ 26 ॥ sadānandapūrṇā svātmaiva paradevatā lalitā ॥ 27 ॥

lauhityametasya sarvasya vimarśaḥ ॥ 28 ॥

That which cannot be contained in form, that which is one's innermost self, is called Kameshvara. And continually filled with bliss, verily one's own innermost self , that which cannot be fathomed is called Lalita. During deep meditation, the ruddy rosy hue of the Self is seen.

श्री सर्वानन्दमय चक्रं नवमावरणम्

Ninth āvaraṇa navamāvaraṇa नवमावरणम् - sarvānandamayacakra श्री सर्व आनन्द-मय चक्रं

Bindu bindusthāna, red color श्रीं

Śrī Mahātripurasundarī (Śiva-śakty-aikya-rūpiṇī)

श्रीललिता महा त्रिपुर सुंदर्यै नमः

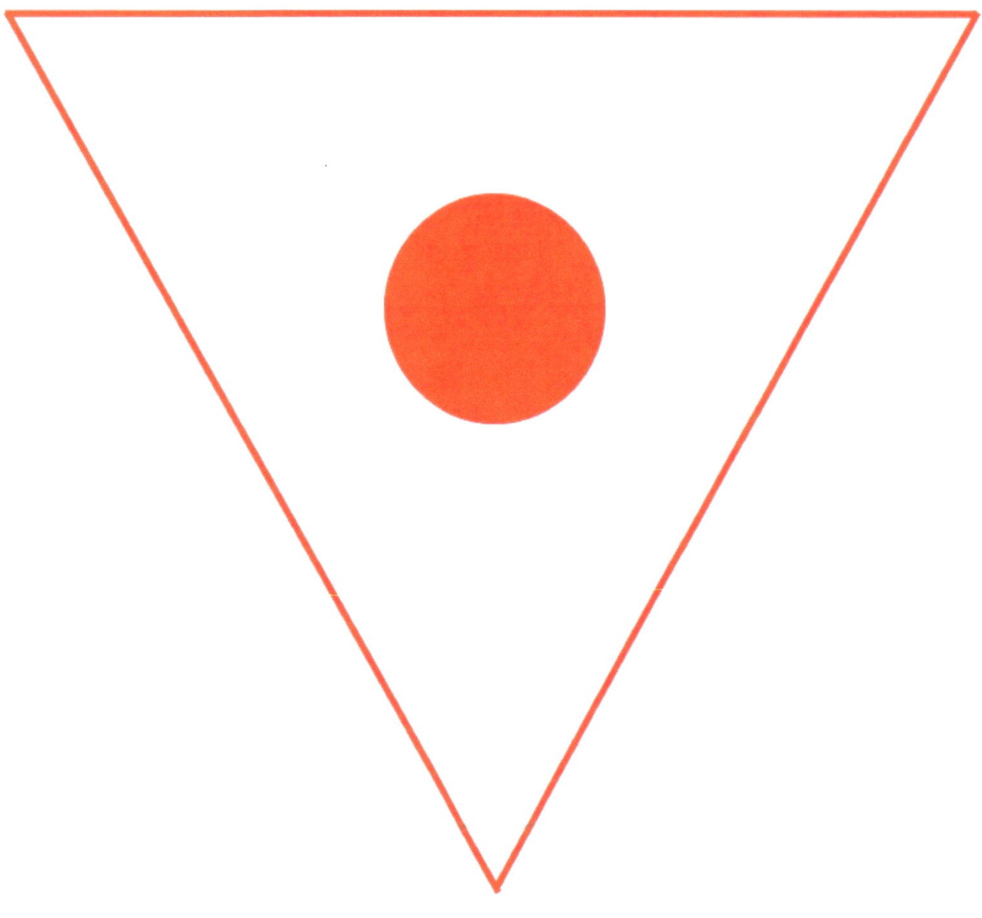

Sri Yantra

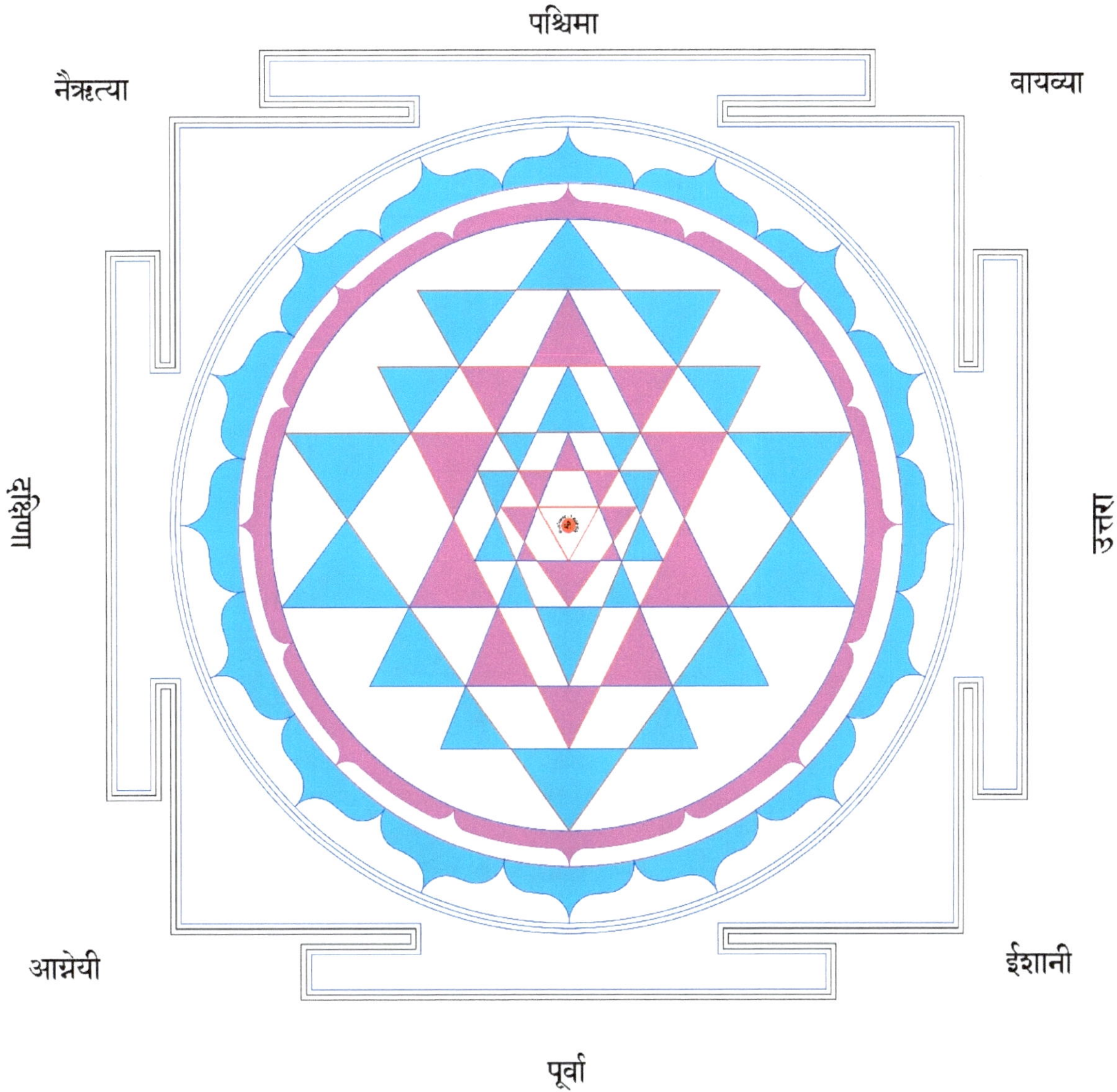

9th Enclosure – Innermost Dot = बिन्दु Bindu श्री सर्वानन्दमय चक्रं नवमावरणम्

Become Still, Silent, Soft, Melted, Absorbed in Divine Union.

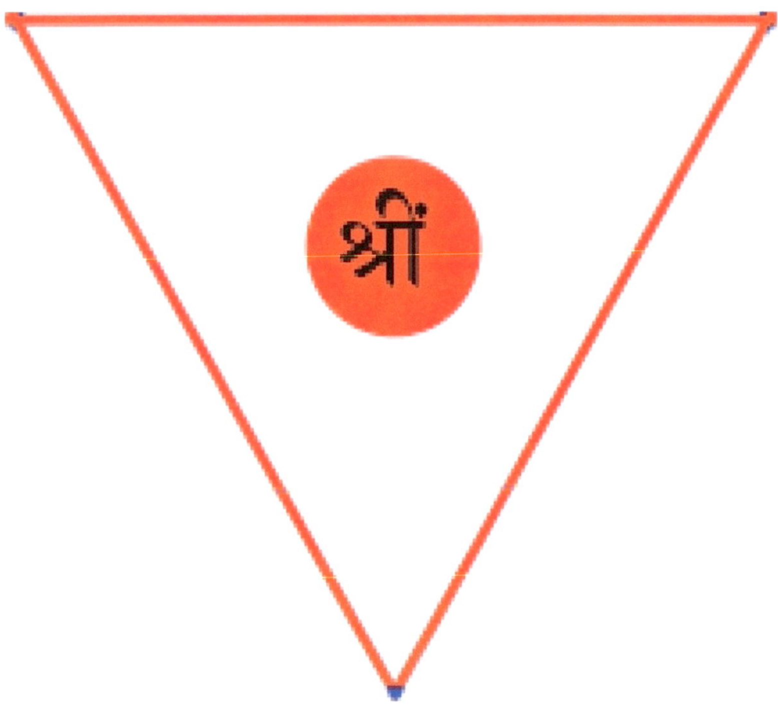

Sri Yantra Complete

॥ ॐ श्री ललिता महात्रिपुरसुन्दर्यै नमः ॥

श्री यन्त्रम्

Sri Yantra Complete with Inscriptions

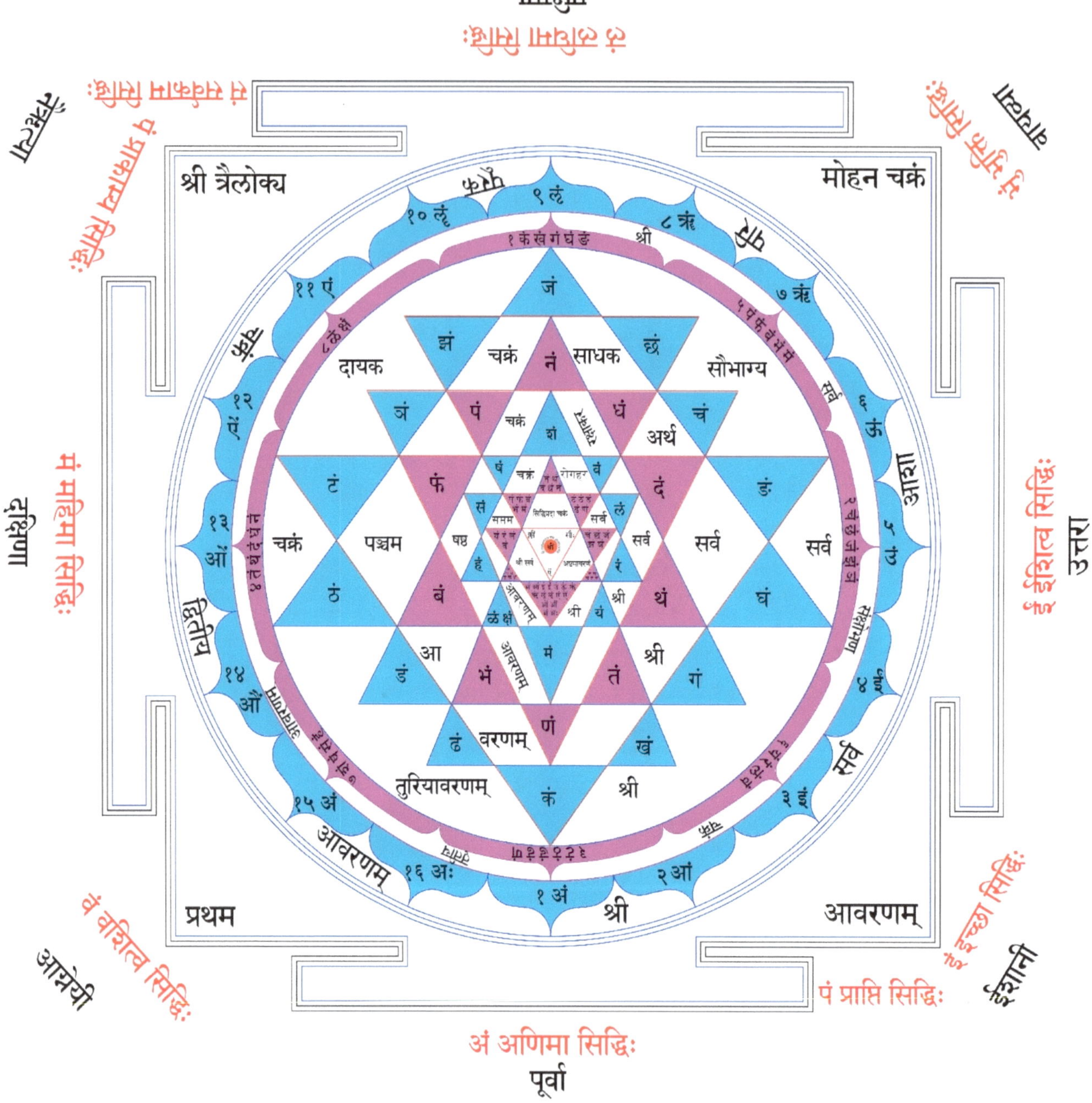

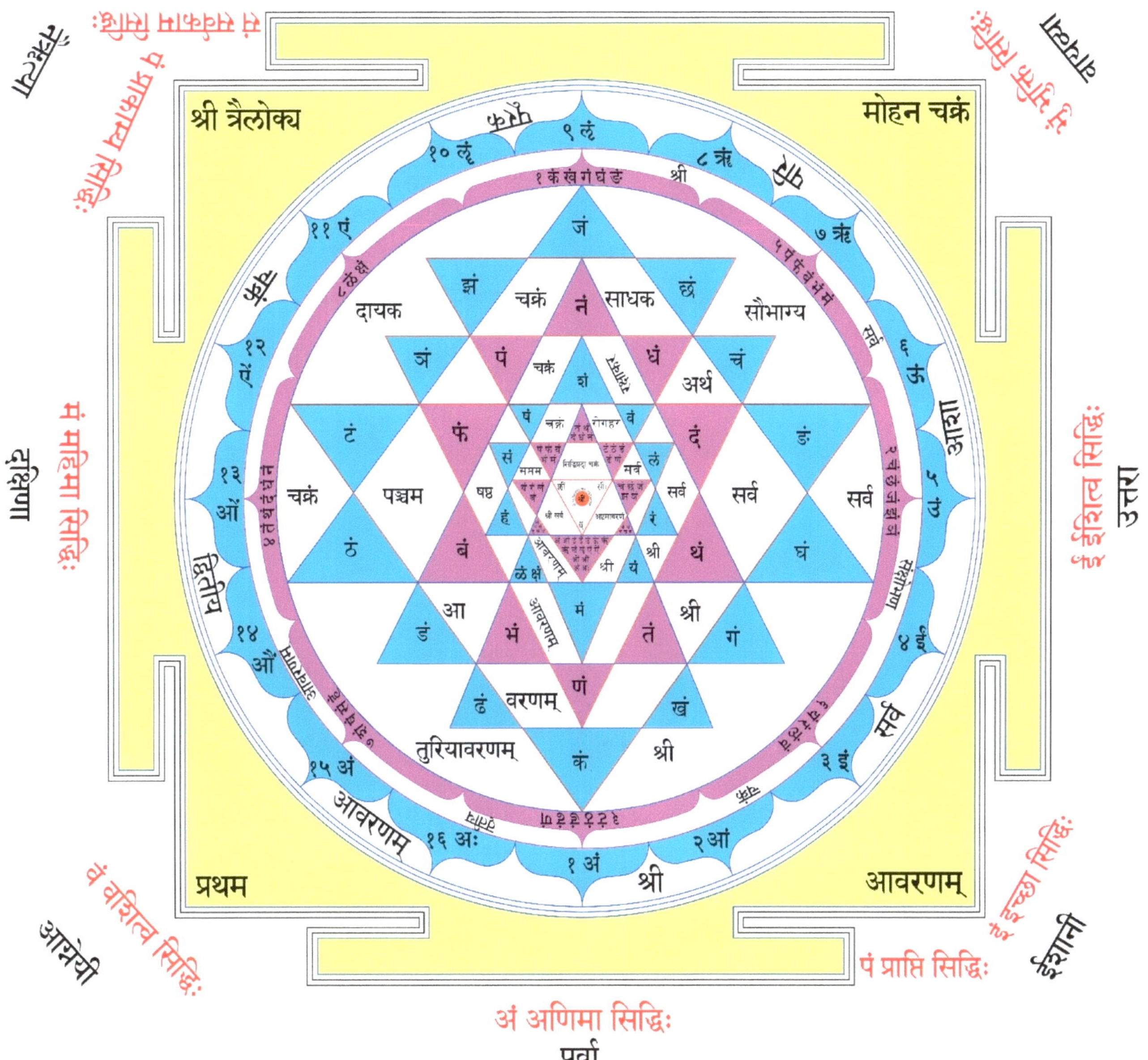

॥ ॐ श्री ललिता महात्रिपुरसुन्दर्यै नमः ॥

श्री यन्त्रम्

Sandhi Points 24 Dual Intersections

The Sri Yantra consists of **dual** intersecting points that are 24 in number. These junctions are known as Sandhi (Joint), where two lines cross each other.

Sri Yantra

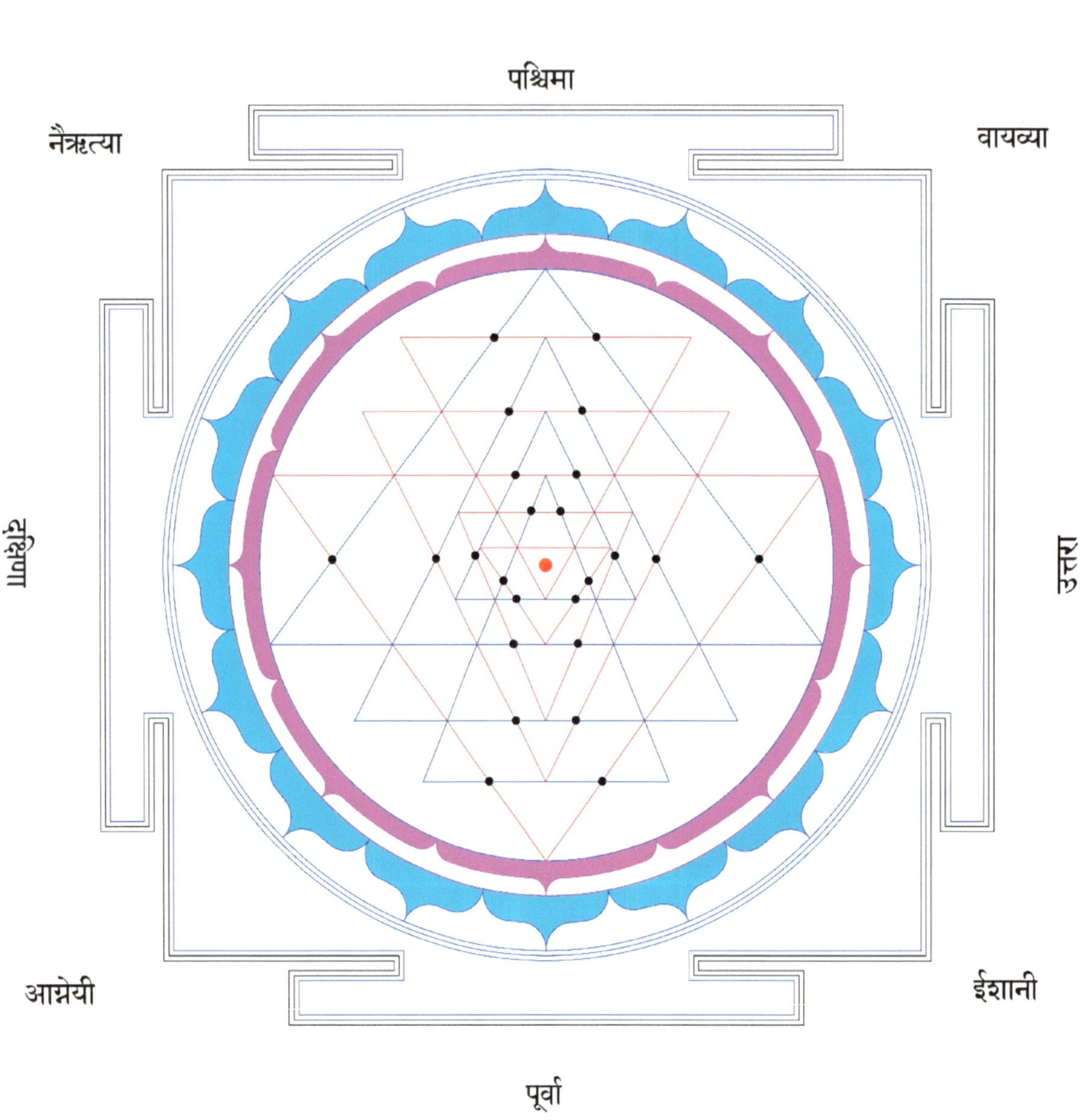

The 24 Sandhi Junctions in the Sri Yantra, shown by dots.

Marma Points 18 Triple Intersections

The Sri Yantra consists of **triple** intersecting points that are 18 in number. These junctions are known as Marma (presence of the divinity), where three lines cross each other.

Sri Yantra

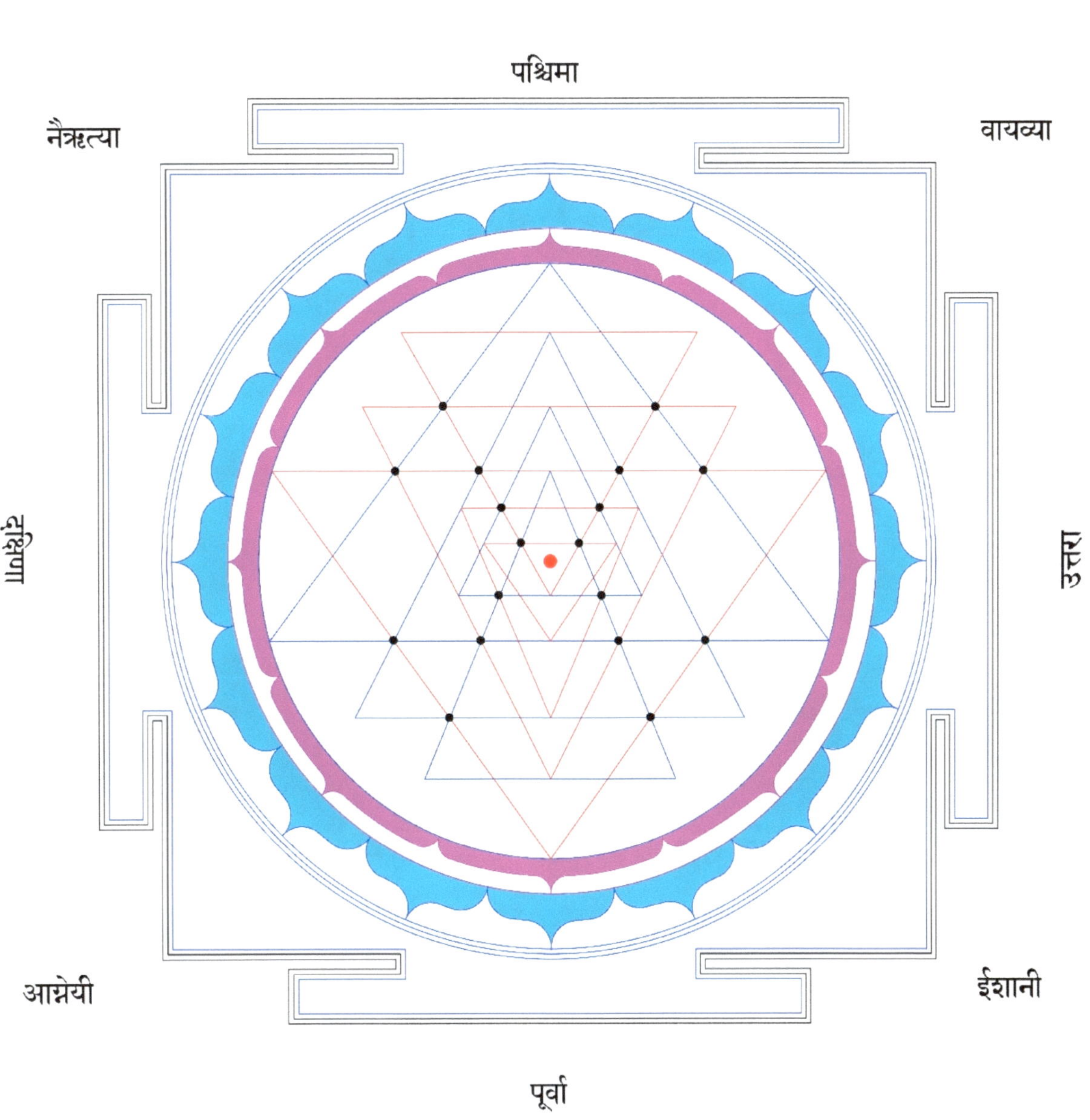

The 18 Marma Junctions in the Sri Yantra, shown by dots.

Some Beautiful Yantras

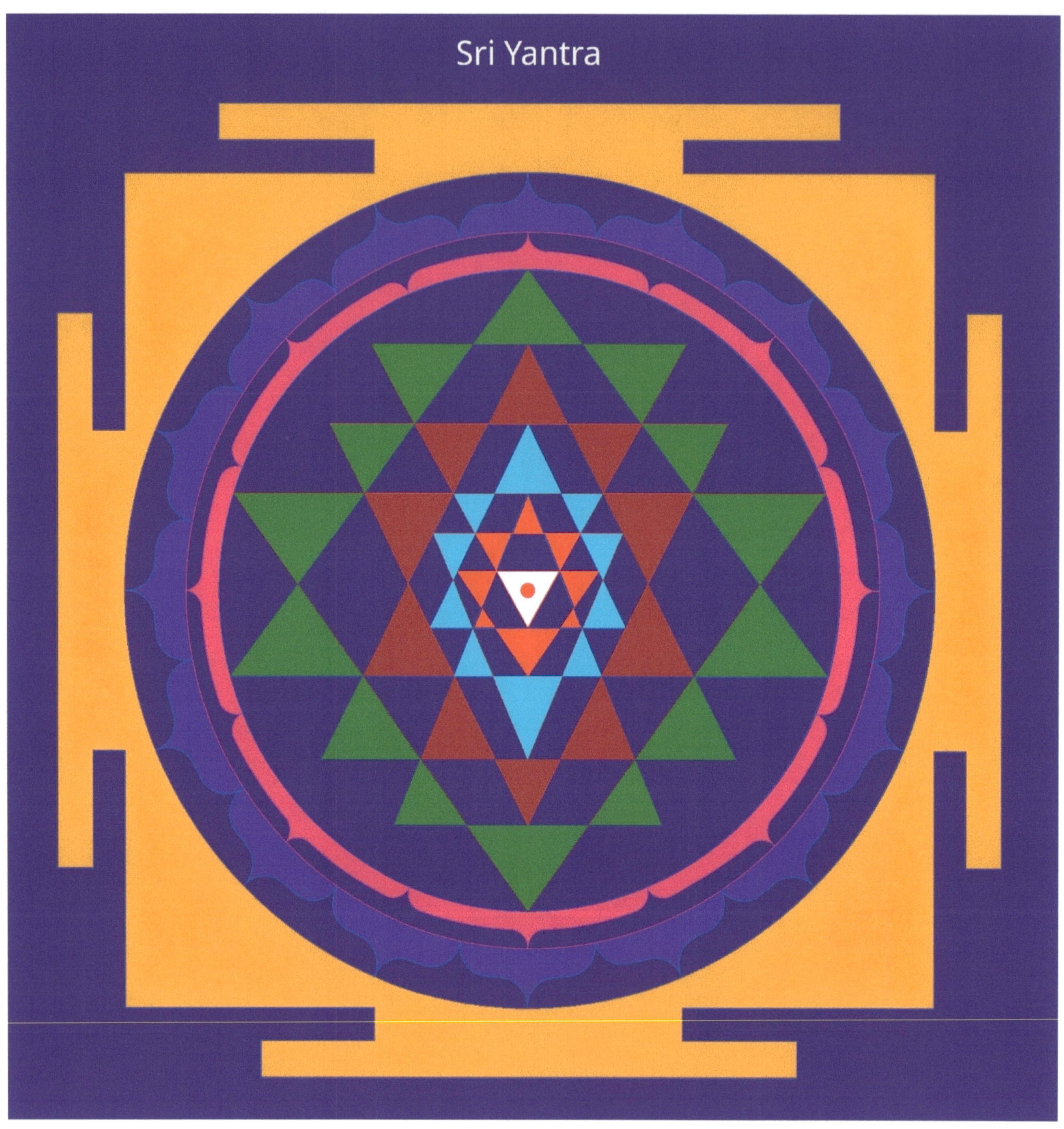

उत्तरा
पूर्वा
॥ ॐ श्री ललिता महात्रिपुरसुन्दर्यै नमः ॥
श्री यन्त्रम्

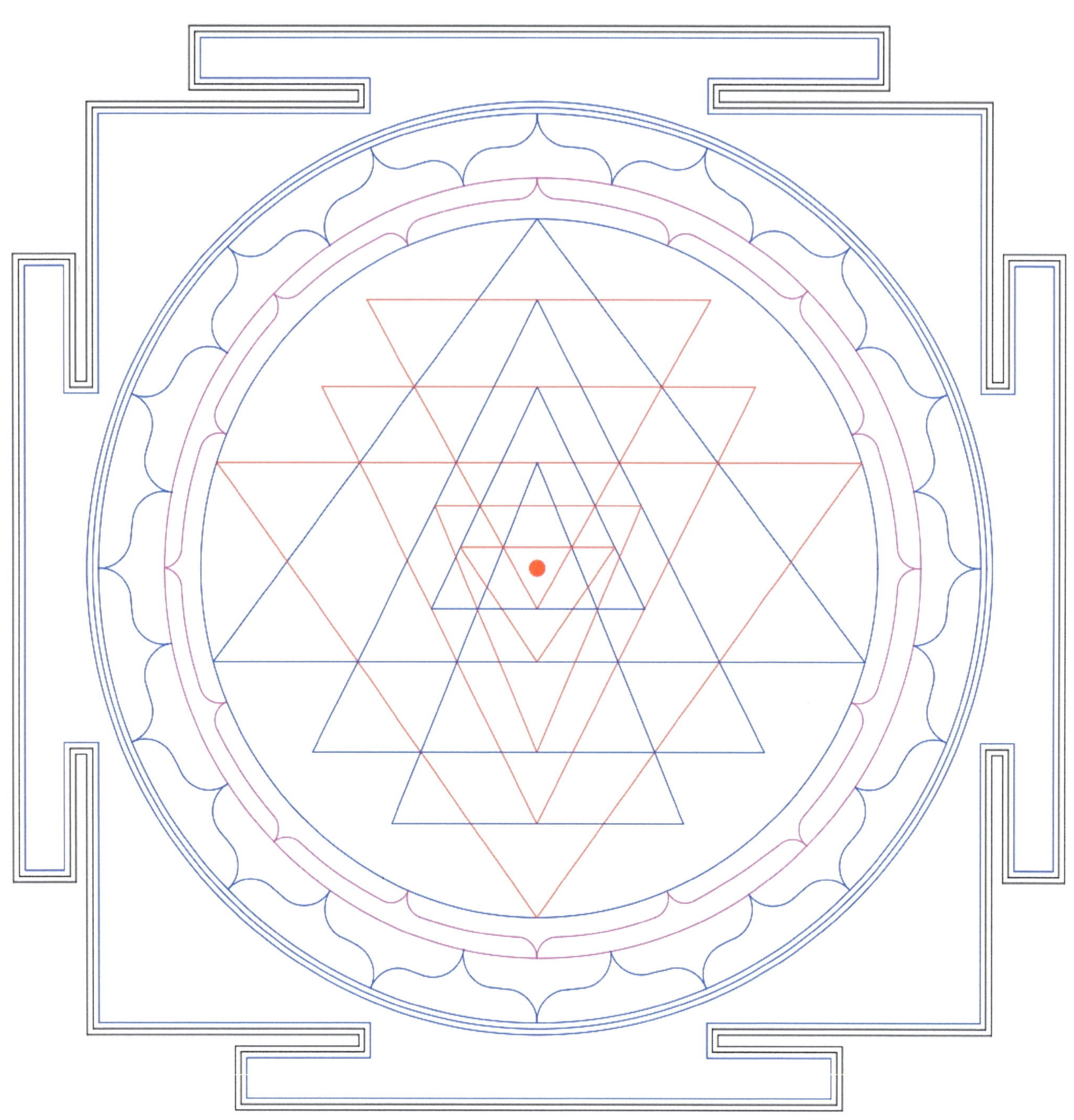

Sri Matrika Chakra Viveka diagram

There is ancient Kashmir Shaivism text on the Sri Chakra, known as the Sri Matrika Chakra Viveka.
It gives copious details on the ritual aspect and spiritual connotation of the Sri Yantra.

1st Enclosure = Yellowish Four sided Gates त्रिकोण चतुरस्र प फ ब भ

2nd Enclosure = Bluish Sixteen Petalled Lotus षोडश-दल पद्म = long आं अं३ ई इं३ ऊ उं३ ऋ लं३ ए ए३ ऐ ऐ३ ओ ओ३ औ औ३

3rd Enclosure = Reddish Eight Petalled Lotus अष्ट-दल पद्म = short vowels अ इ उ ऋ ल अं अः

4th Enclosure = Greenish Fourteen Triangles चतुर्दशार = 14 vowels अ इ उ ऋ ल ए ओ + आ ई ऊ ॠ ॡ ऐ औ

5th Enclosure = Reddish Ten Triangles बहिर्दशार = 10 row consonants क ख ग घ ङ च छ ज झ ञ

6th Enclosure = Bluish Ten Triangles अन्तर्दशार= 10 row consonants ट ठ ड ढ ण त थ द ध न

7th Enclosure = Reddish Eight Triangles अष्टार = 4 semivowels and 4 sibilants य र ल व श ष स ह

8th Enclosure = White Downward facing Triangle त्रिकोण म

9th Enclosure = Red Dot बिन्दु क्ष

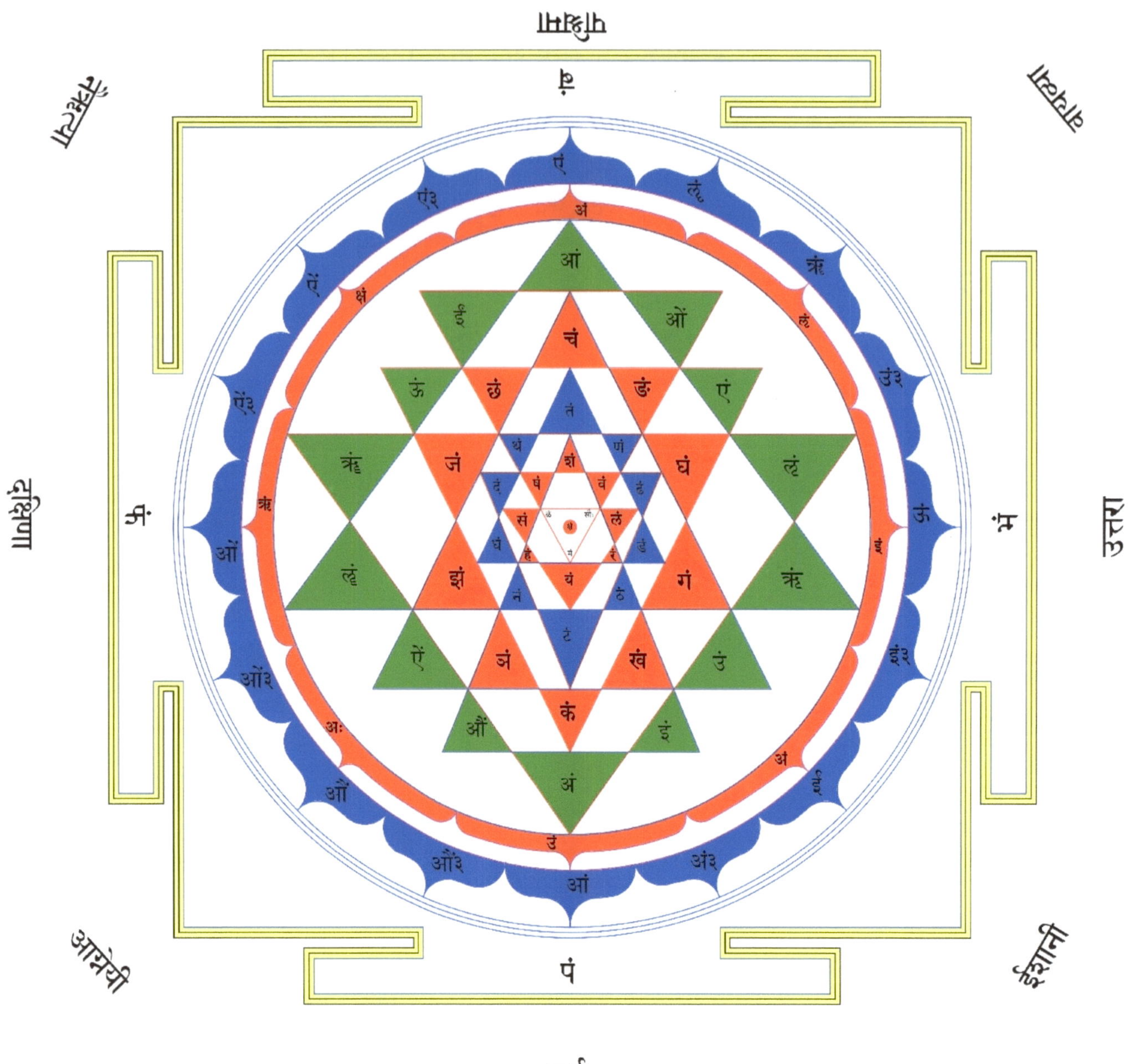

॥ ॐ श्री ललिता महात्रिपुरसुन्दर्यै नमः ॥

श्री यन्त्रम्

Golden Ratio Triangle in Sri Yantra

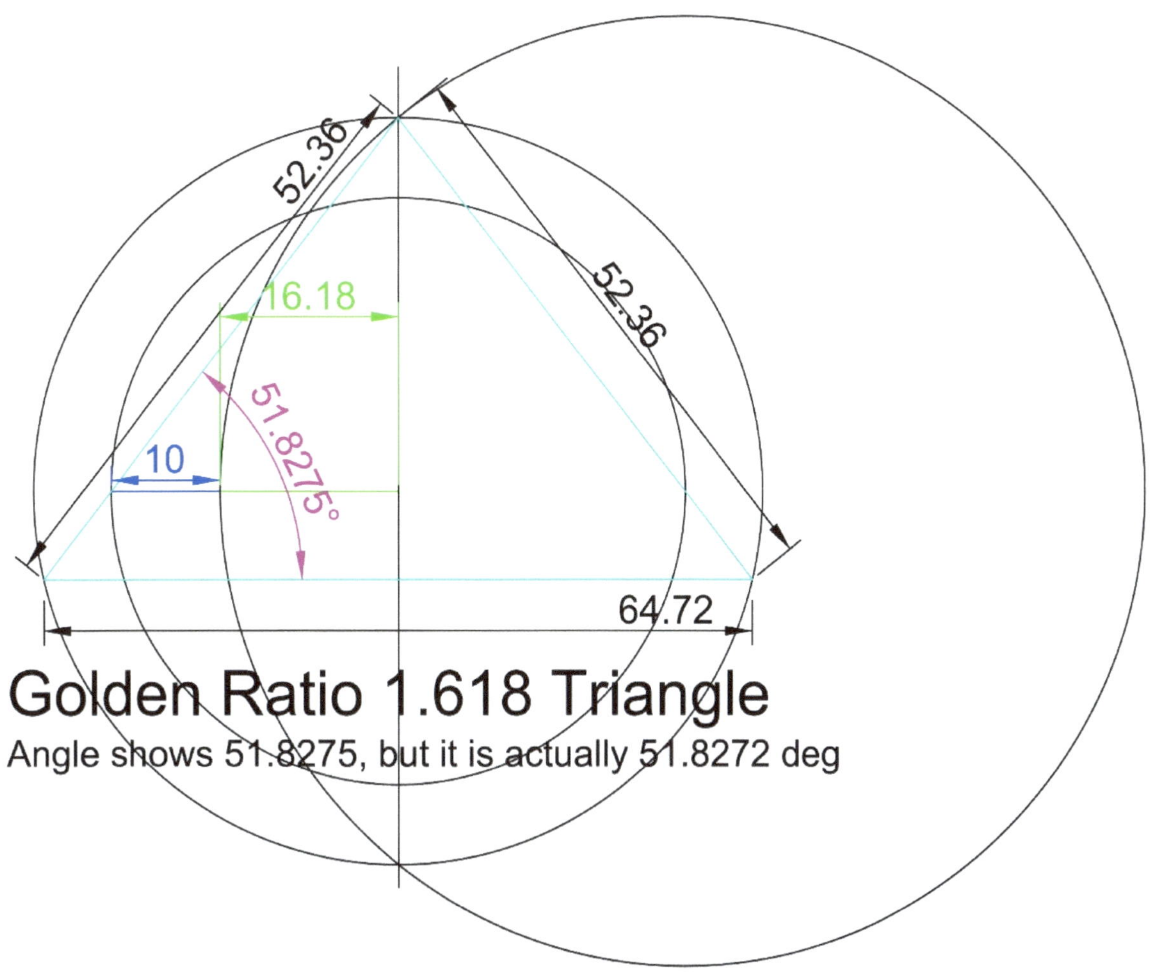

The biggest 1st Upward Apex Triangle in the Sri Yantra is built using the Golden Ratio found in nature.

What is the Golden Ratio? First let us see the Fibonacci series.

The Fibonacci numbers are **integers** in the following sequence: **0, 1, 1, 2, 3, 5, 8, 13, 21, 34, 55, 89, 144**..i.e., a series of numbers in which the next number is made by adding the previous two integers.

Now let us see the ratio of two successive fibonacci numbers.

i.	1/0	invalid
ii.	1/1 = 1	
iii.	2/1 = 2	
iv.	3/2 = 1.5	
v.	5/3 = 1.6666	
vi.	8/5 = 1.6	
vii.	13/8 = 1.625	
viii.	21/13 = 1.6153	
ix.	34/21 = 1.6190	
x.	55/34 = 1.6176	

xi.   89/55 = 1.6181
xii.   144/89 = 1.6179
xiii.   233/144 = 1.6180
xiv.   377/233 = 1.6180
xv.   610/377 = 1.6180

After a while this ratio series becomes more or less stable on the irrational number 1.6180, and this number is known as the Golden Ratio.

It is also called the golden section, golden mean, or divine proportion. In mathematics, the irrational number (1 + Square root of 5)/2, often denoted by the Greek letter Phi ϕ, which is approximately equal to 1.618. Thus Golden Ratio = 1.6180 = $(1 + \sqrt{5})/2 = \phi$

Now consider the inverse $1/\phi$ = 0.6180 = ϕ -1 which is called phi and denoted by φ (lowercase).

a + b = 0.618 + 1 = 1.6180 = Phi = ϕ = Uppercase.

0.6180 = phi = φ = Lowercase.

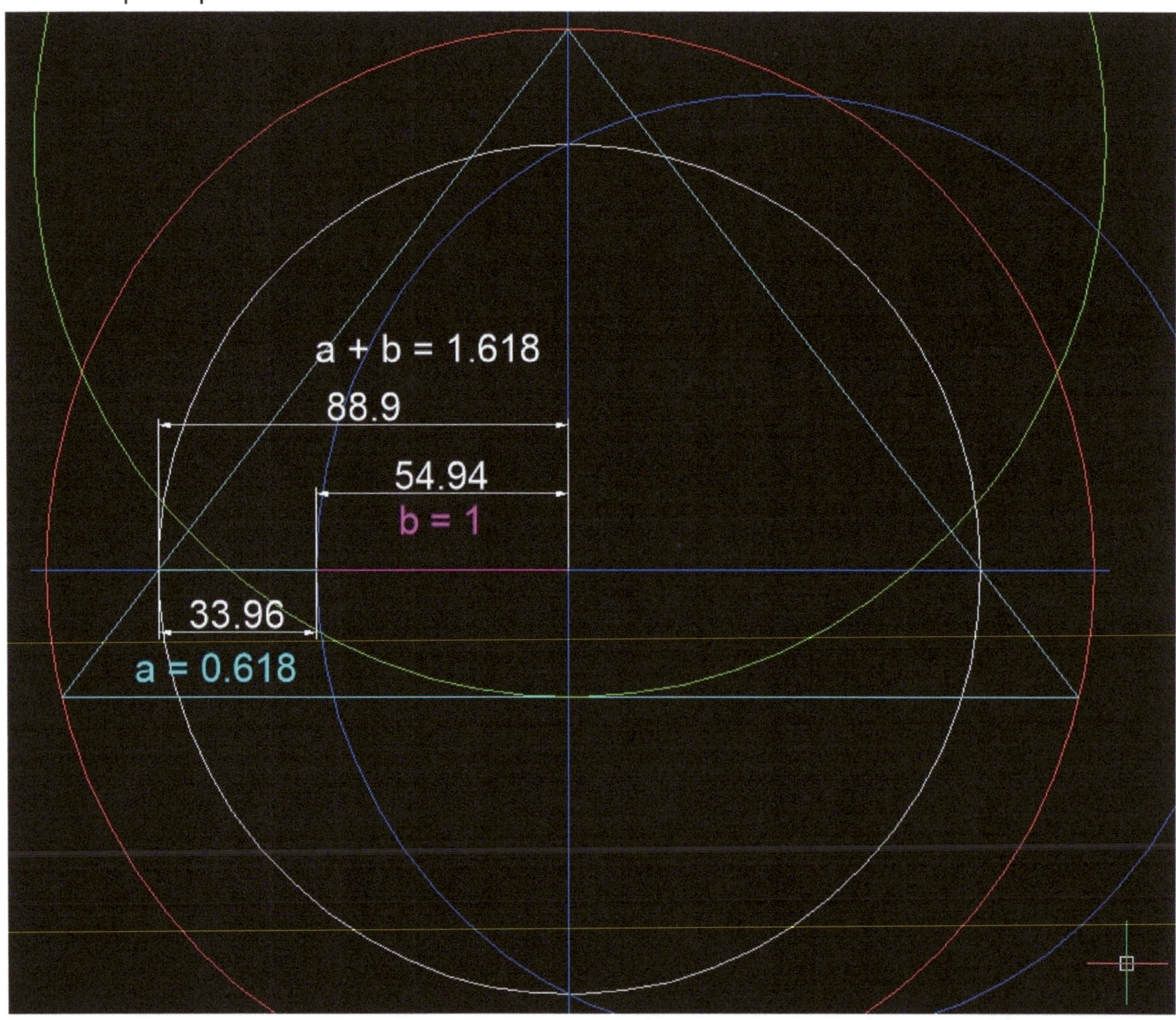

Golden Ratio Triangle in the Great Pyramid of Giza

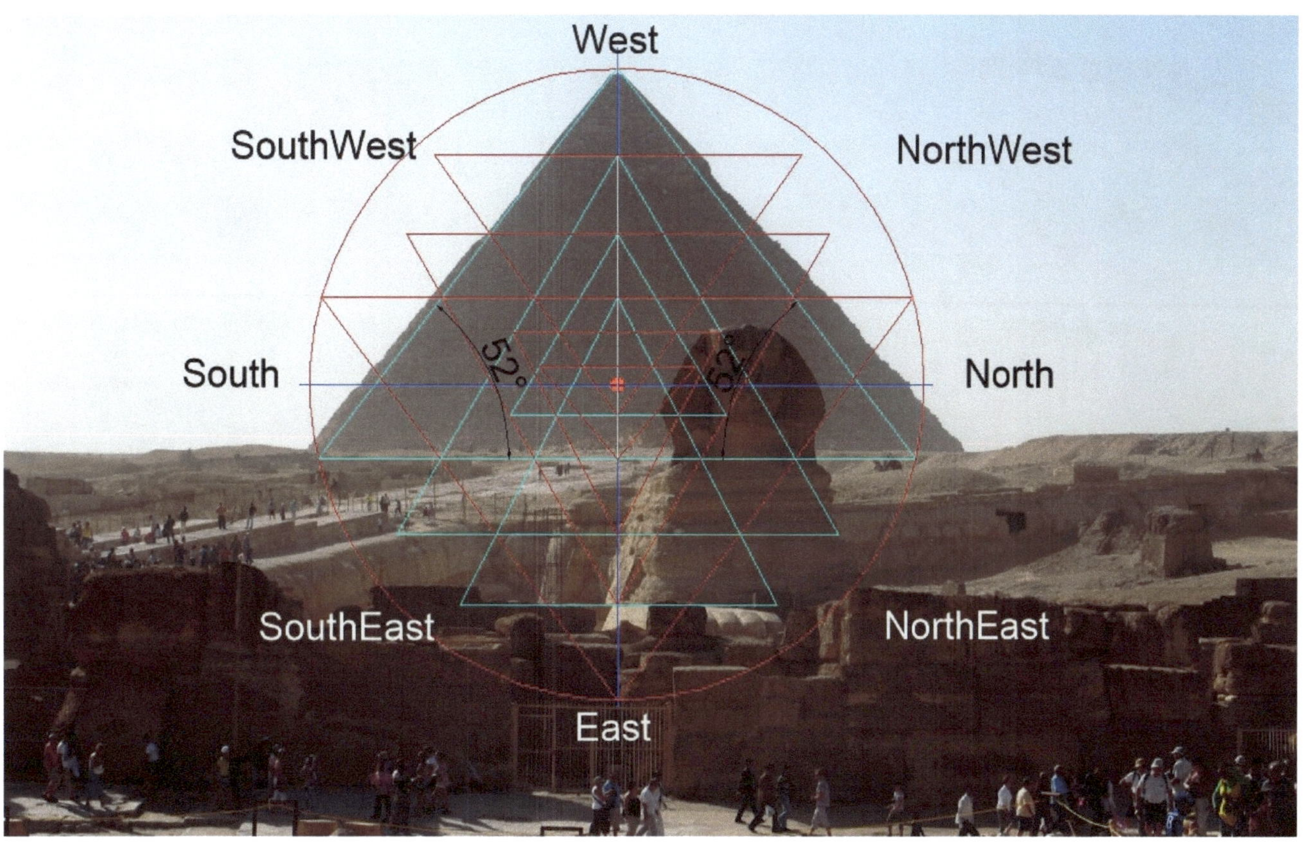

Golden Ratio Triangle as seen in Creation

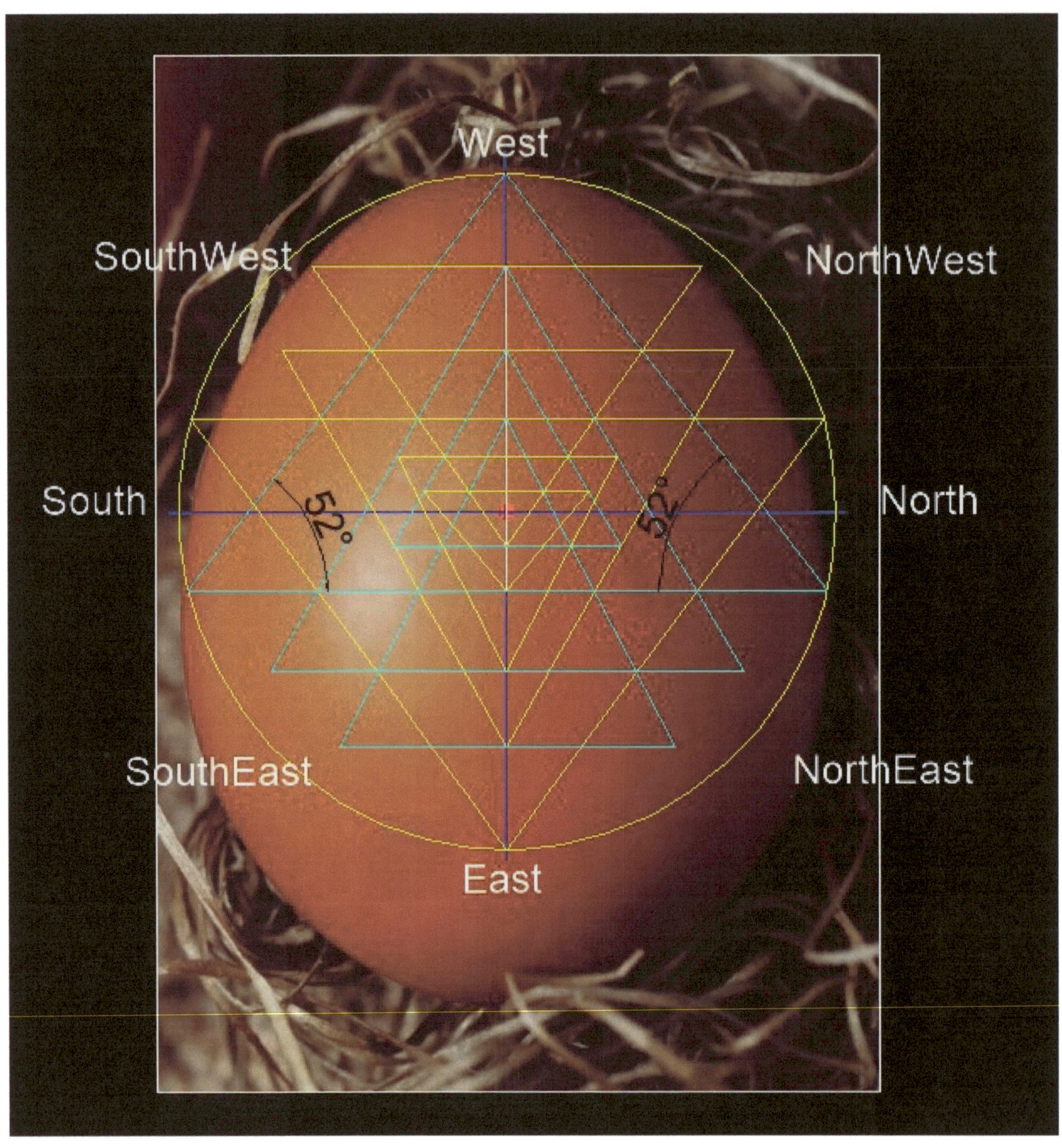

Golden ratio Triangle superimposed on an egg.
Note: The famous Yin Yang symbol (Tai Chi) is also drawn in the golden ratio spiral.

Golden ratio Triangle superimposed on human brain.

Golden Ratio vis-à-vis the Vitruvian Man

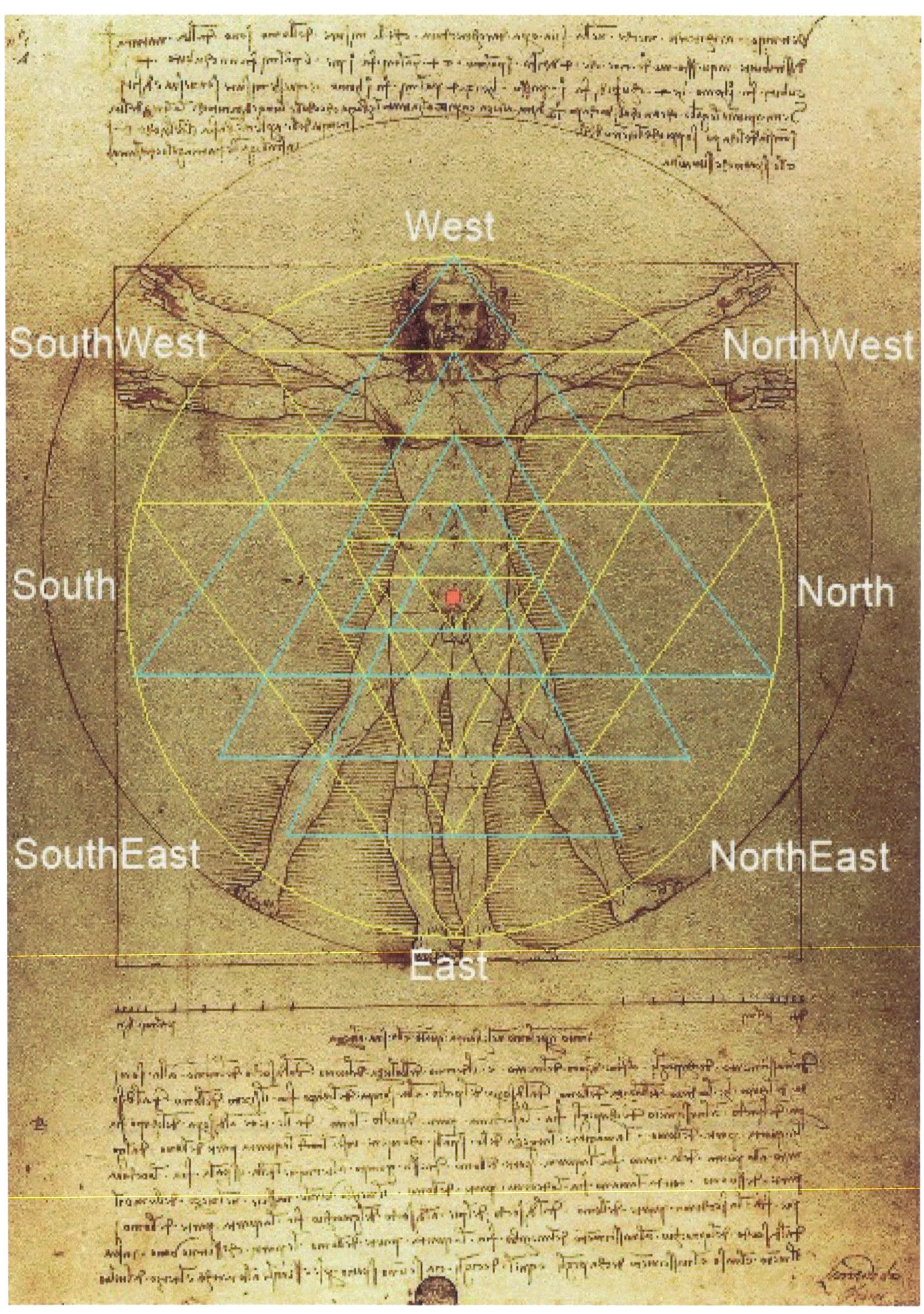

Steps to Draw a Sri Yantra using AutoCad

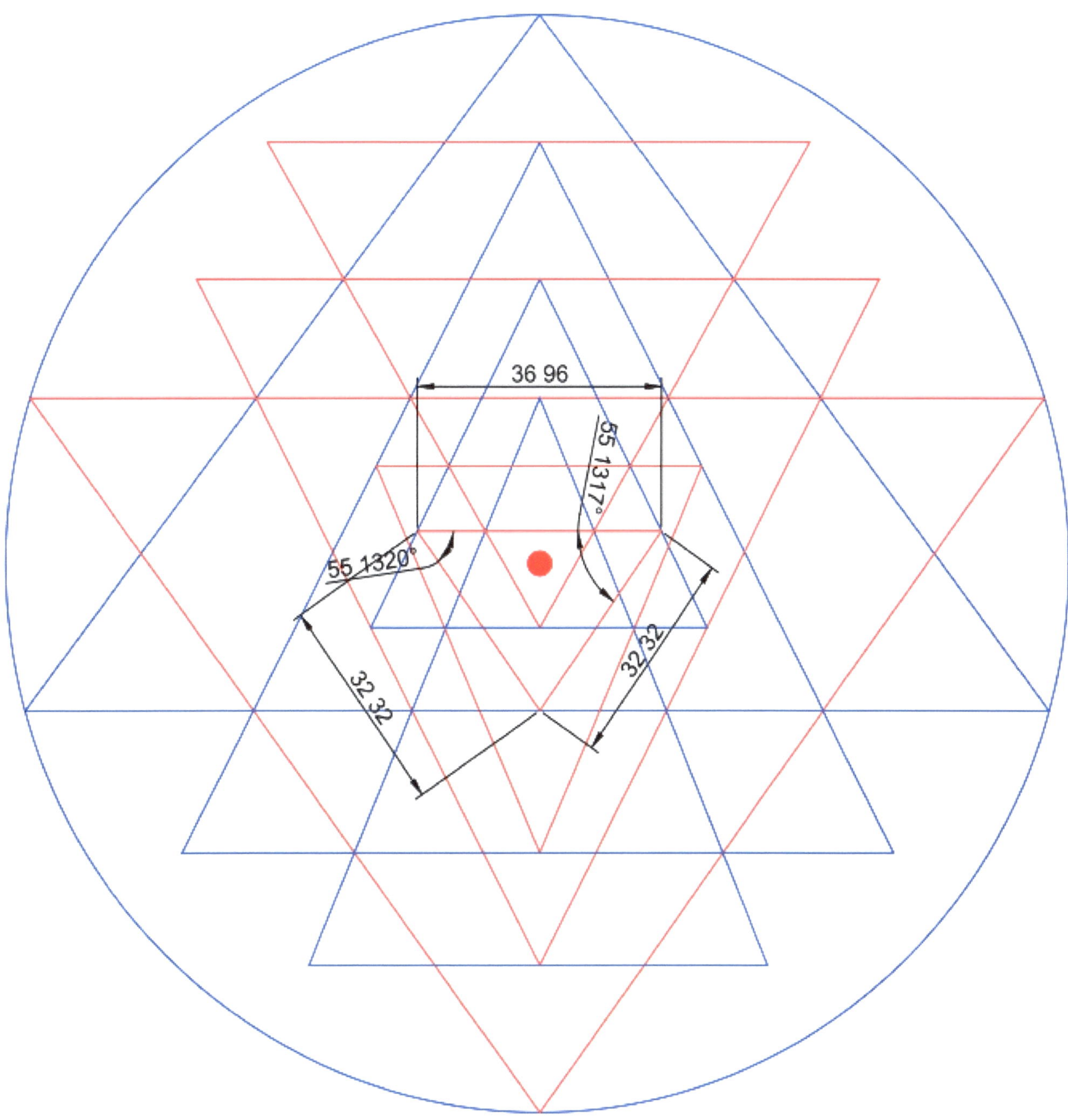

Dimensions of Innermost Downward Triangle

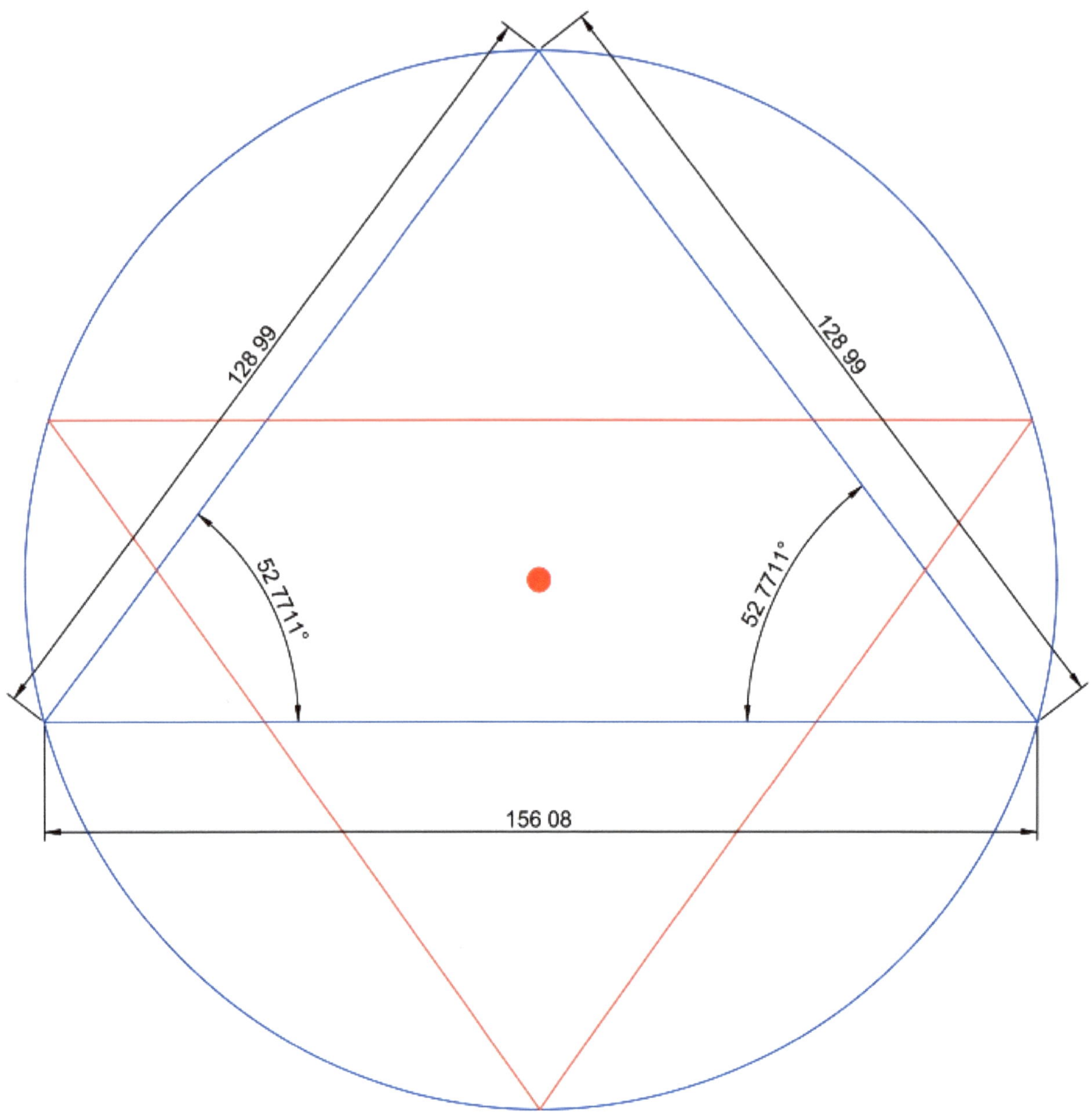

Dimensions of Outermost Upward Apex Triangle

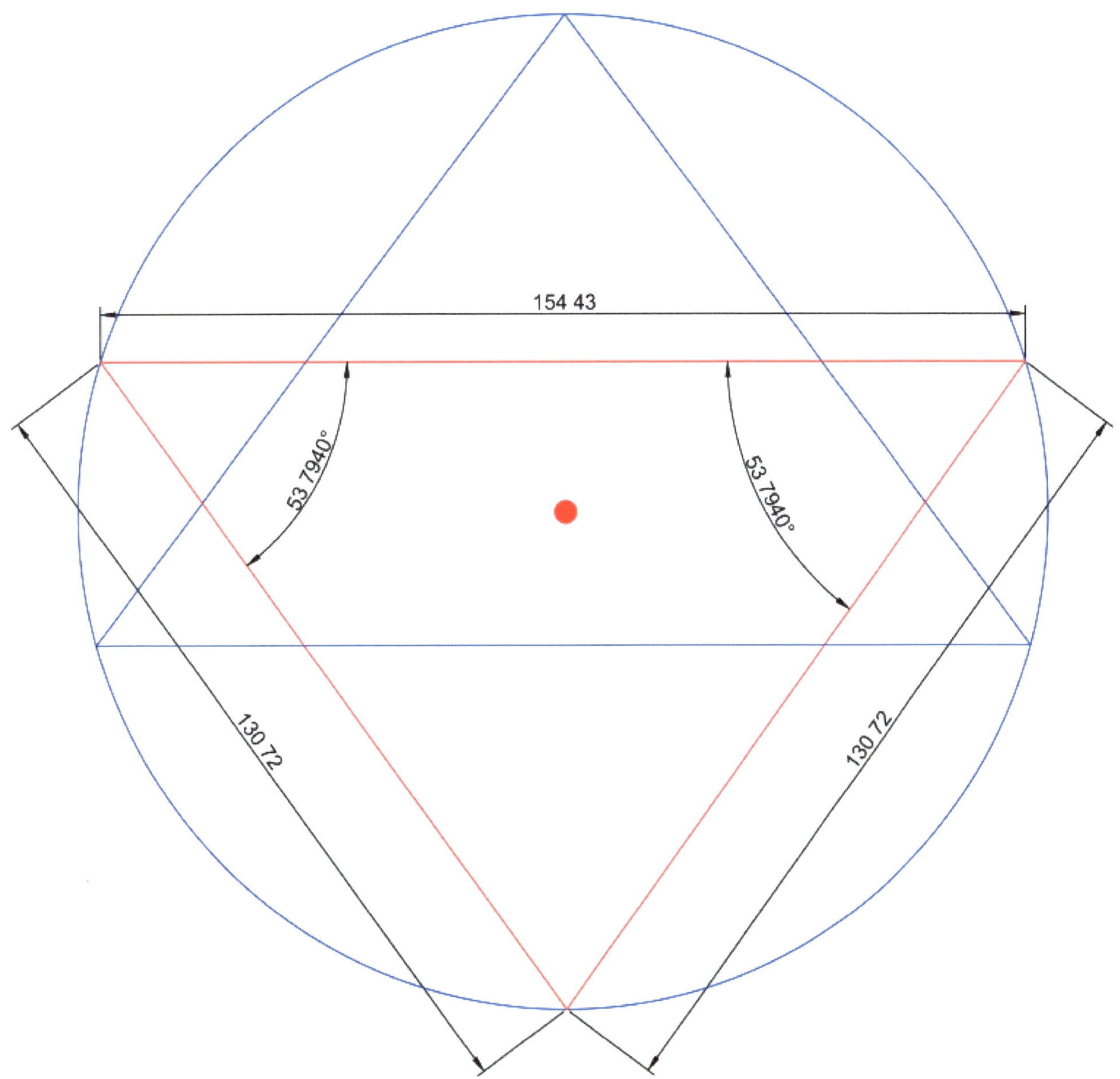

Dimensions of Outermost Downward Apex Triangle

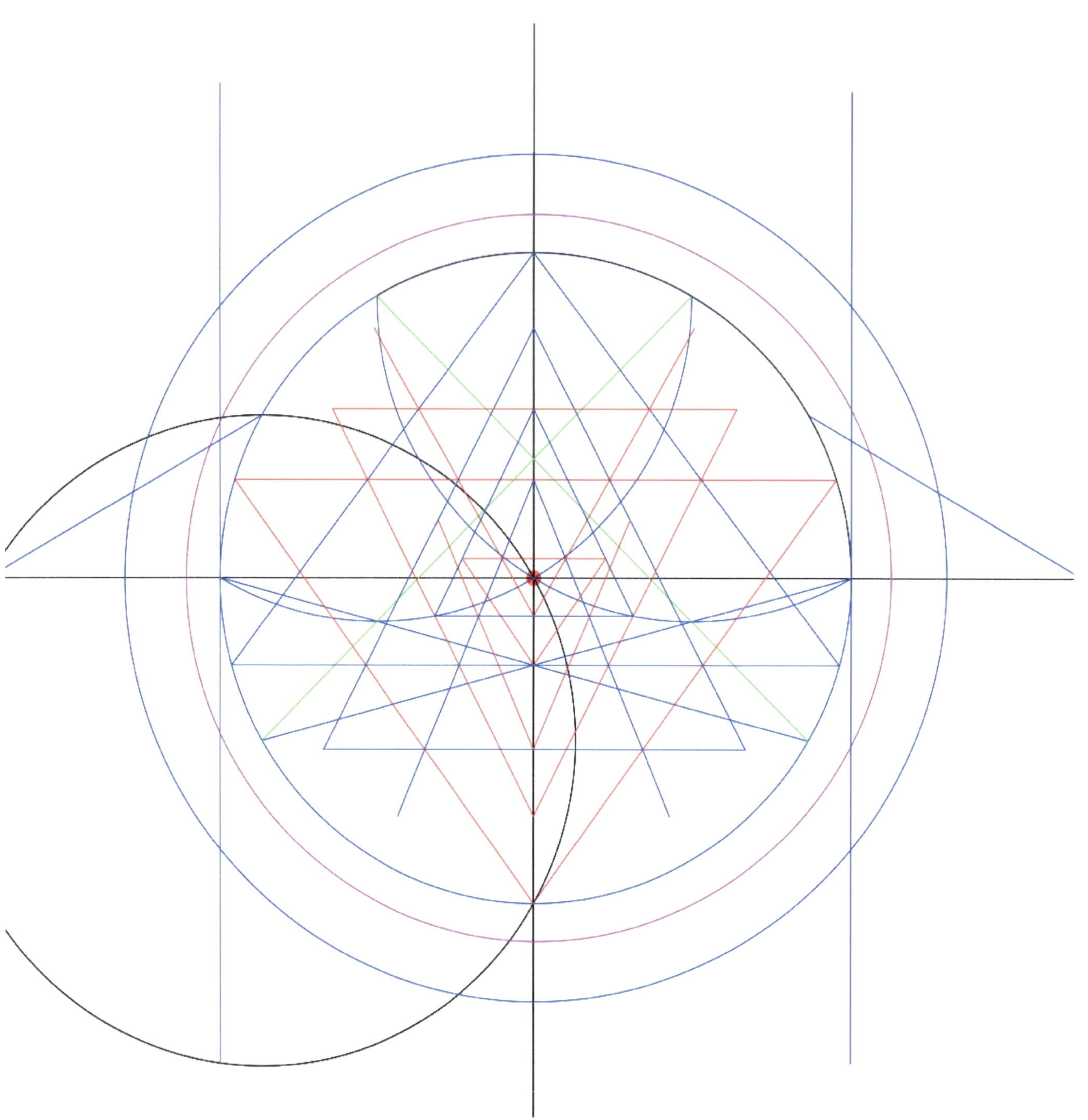

1. Begin with circle Radius 88.9 and center mark

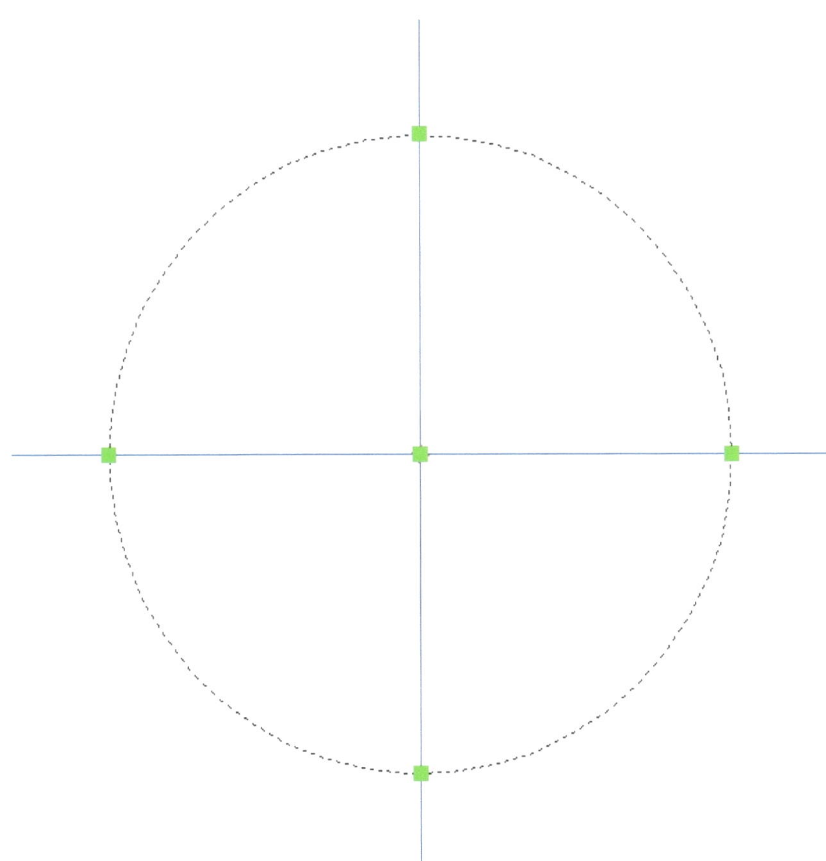

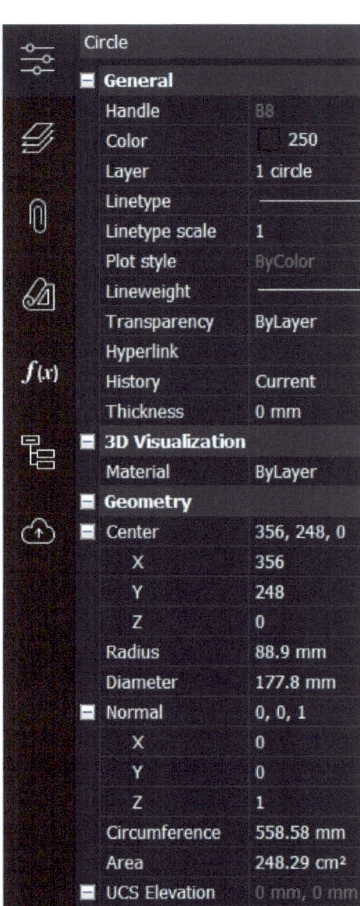

2. Draw two more Circles of same radius 88.9mm and center mark at edge of diameter on horizontal.

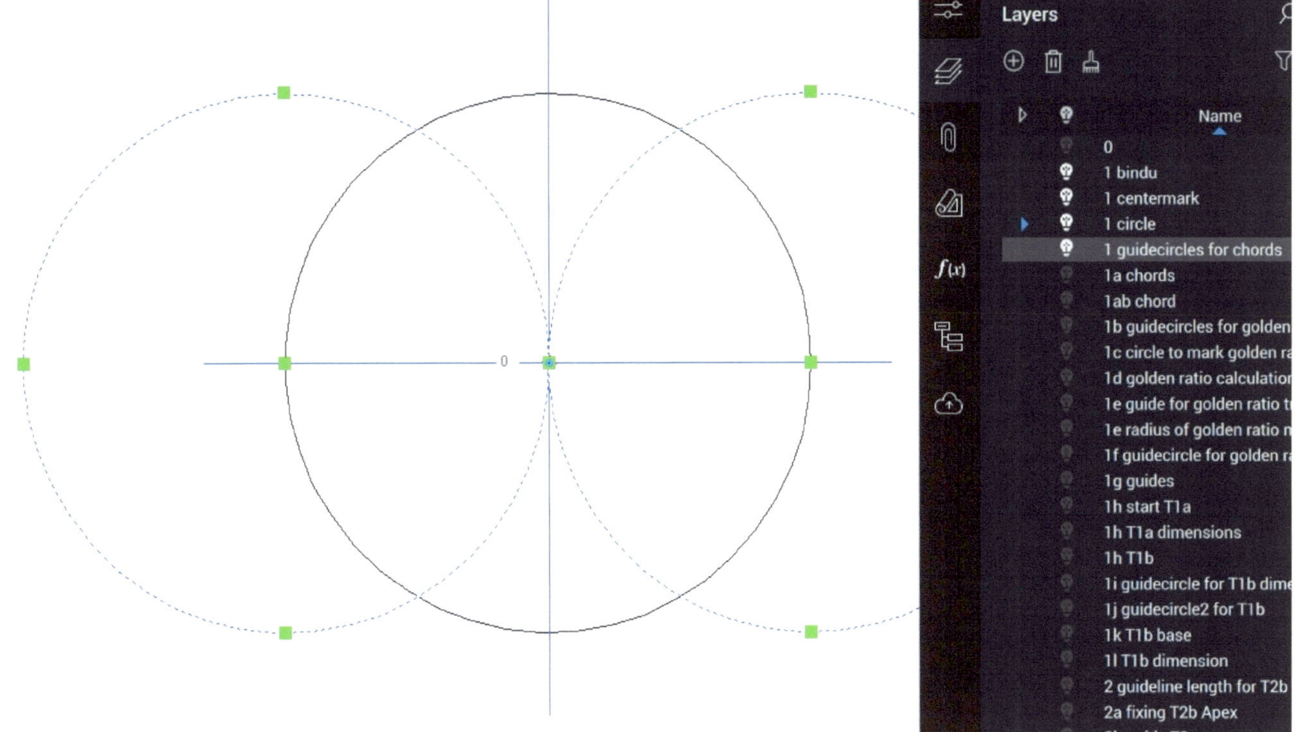

3. Draw vertical chords to mark the intersection of the circles.

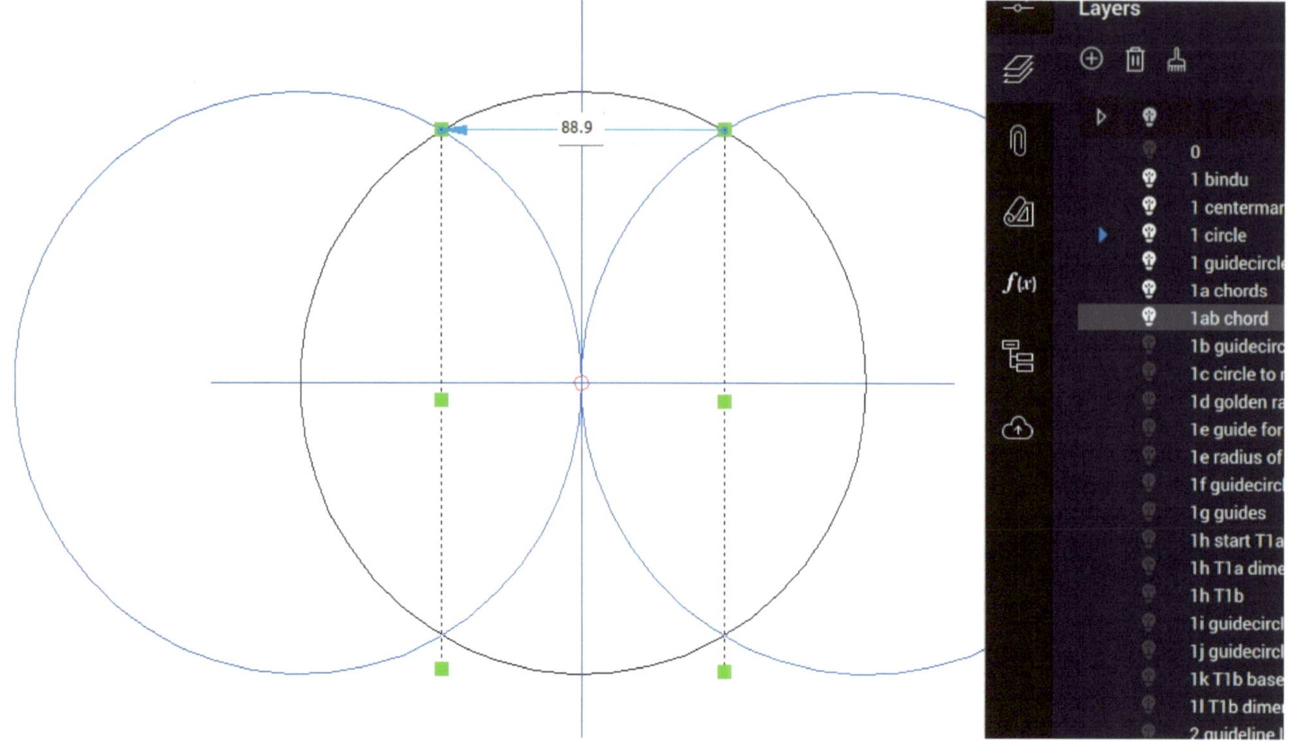

4. Draw two more circles with radius = point where chord bisects the horizontal , and center point on horizontal edge of first circle.

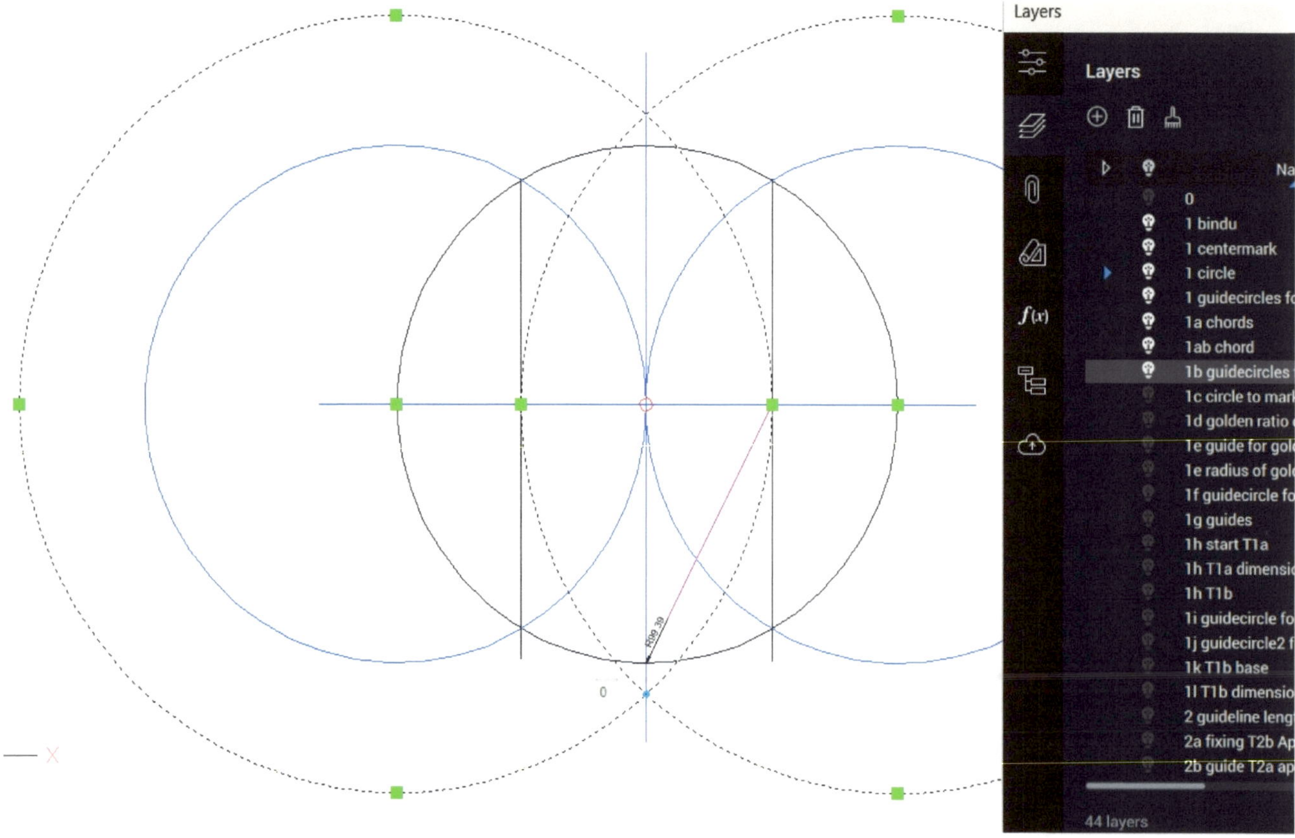

4. Radius of these two new circles = 133.35mm

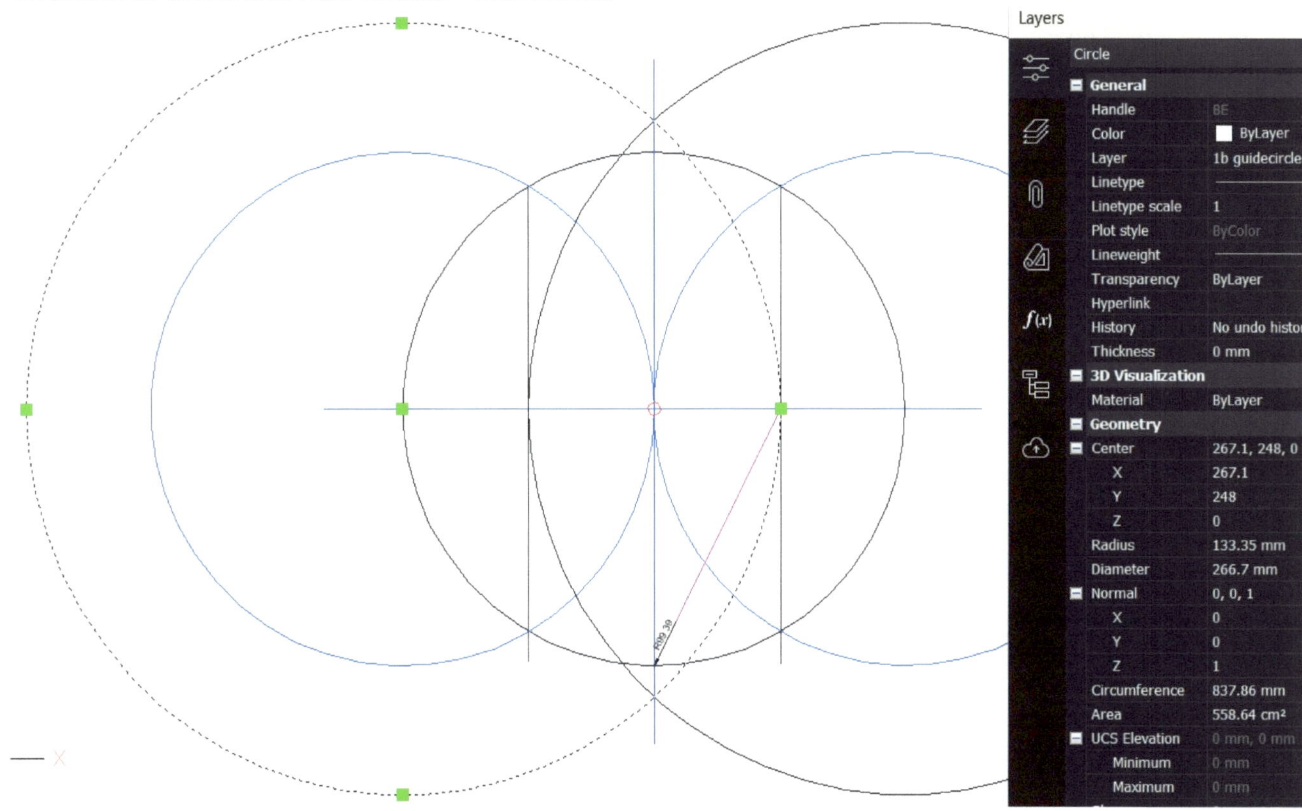

4. Draw another circle of Radius 99.39mm with center point on the intersection of the chord with the horizontal.

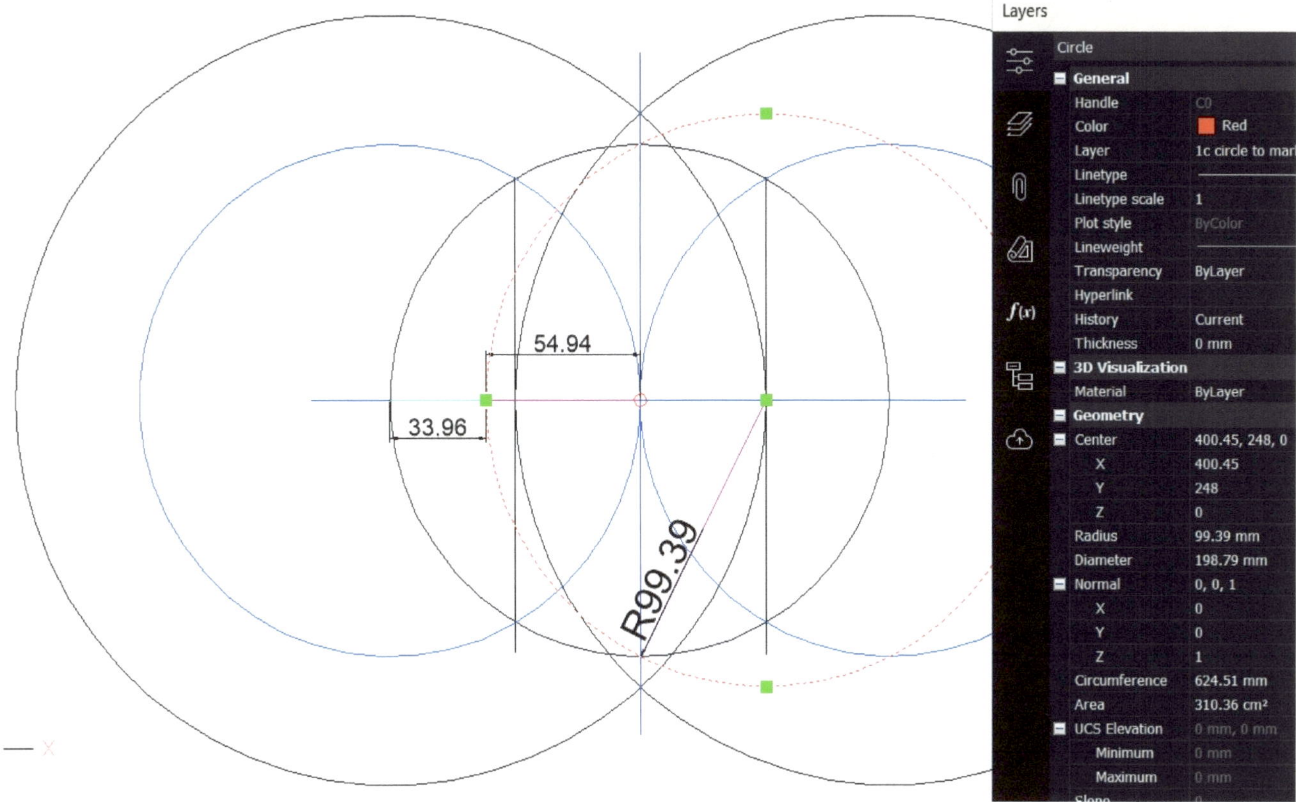

5. This red circle where it intersects the horizontal gives us the marking for the Golden Ratio.
As seen cyan length = 33.96mm, magenta length = 54.94mm.

54.94/33.96 = 1.618 = Phi ϕ the Golden Ratio.

6. Draw a new circle with center on the horizontal edge, and radius of 143.84mm. Notice where it intersects the blue vertical line.

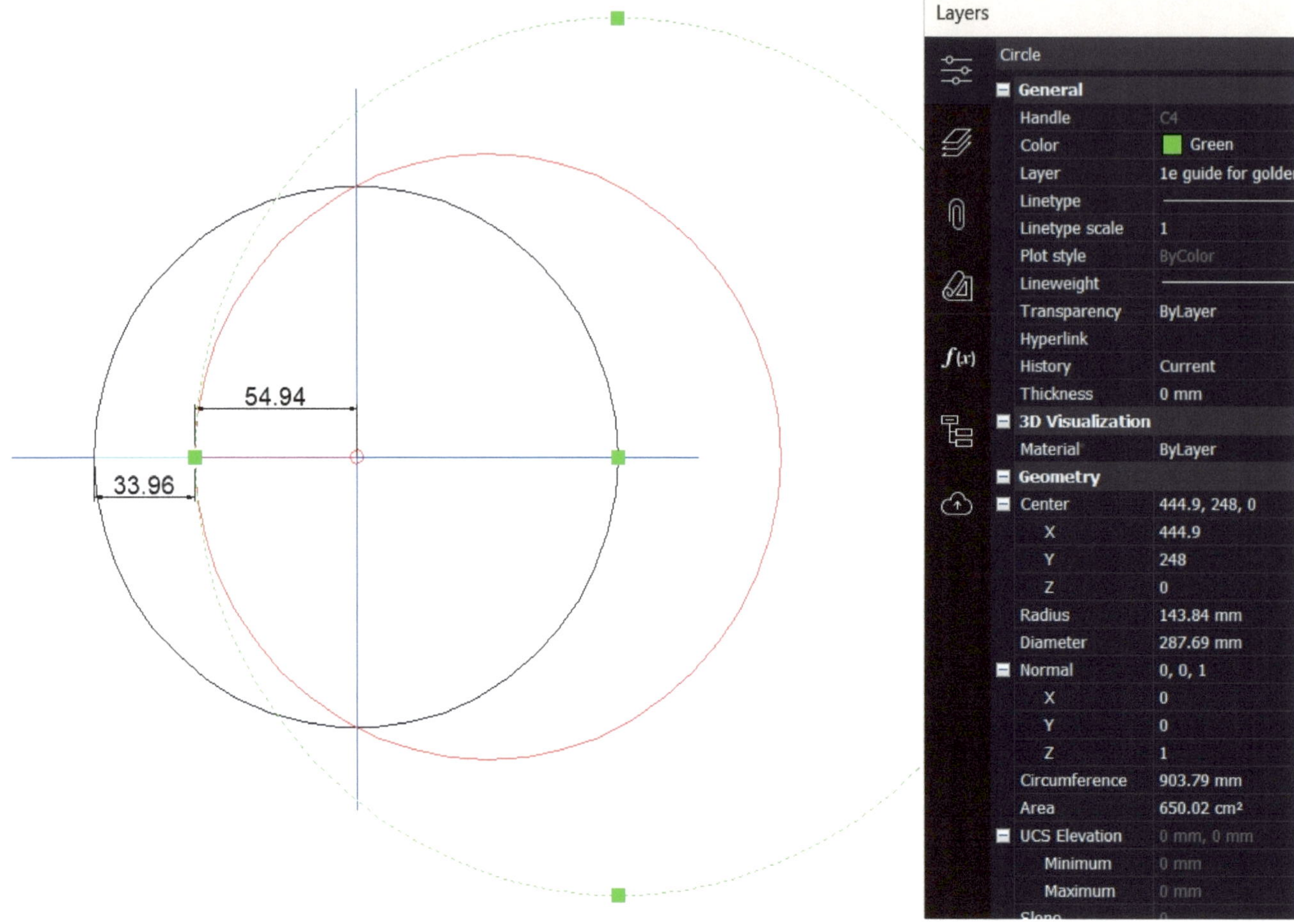

7. Draw a new circle with radius = 113.08mm, using the original center and radius where the green circle intersects the blue vertical.

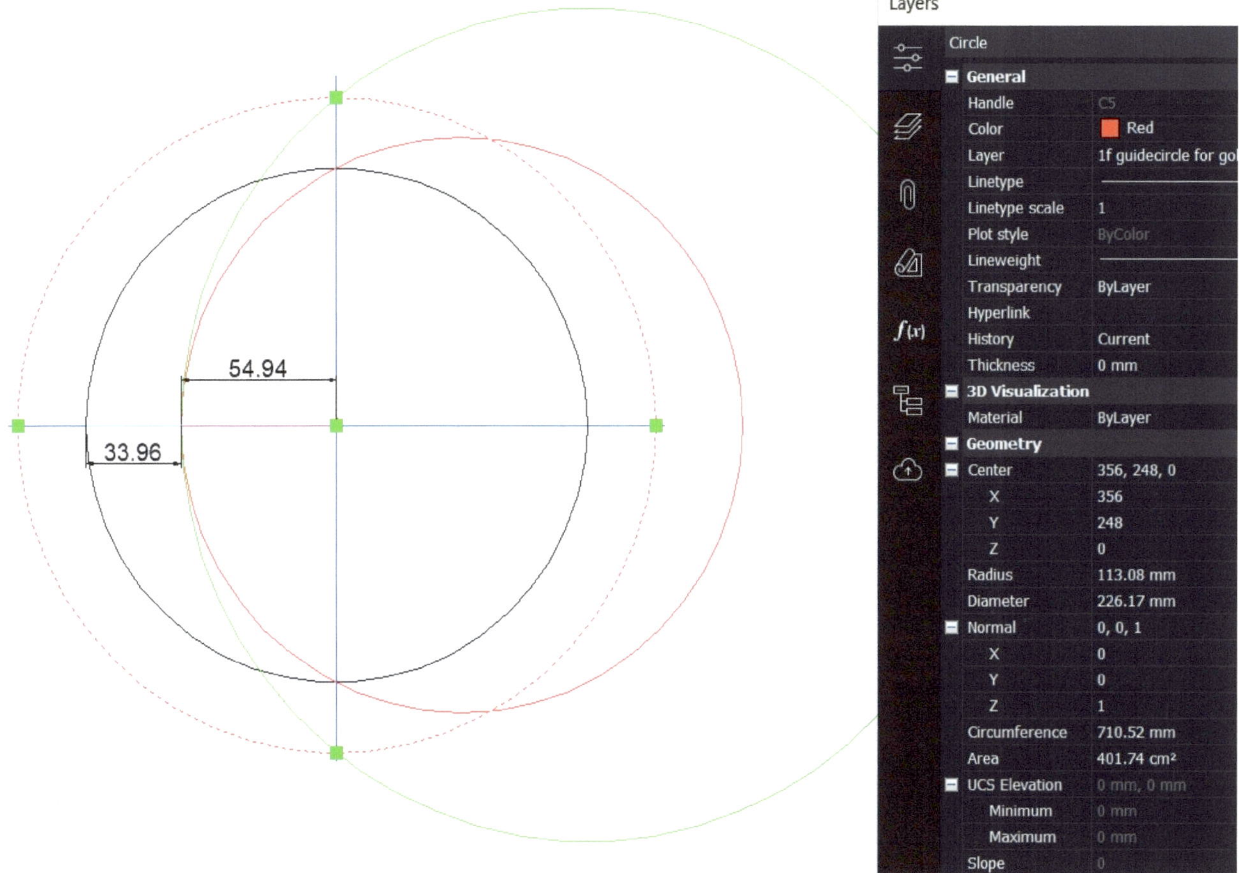

8. This becomes our starting circle for the Sri Yantra, i.e., with a radius of 113.08mm

9. Draw a line of length 177.8mm. Use its start point on the vertical, and the end point on the red circle, and crossing through the intersection of the horizontal with the white circle.
Similarly draw on the other side. This gives us the sides of the Upward Apex Golden Ratio Triangle.

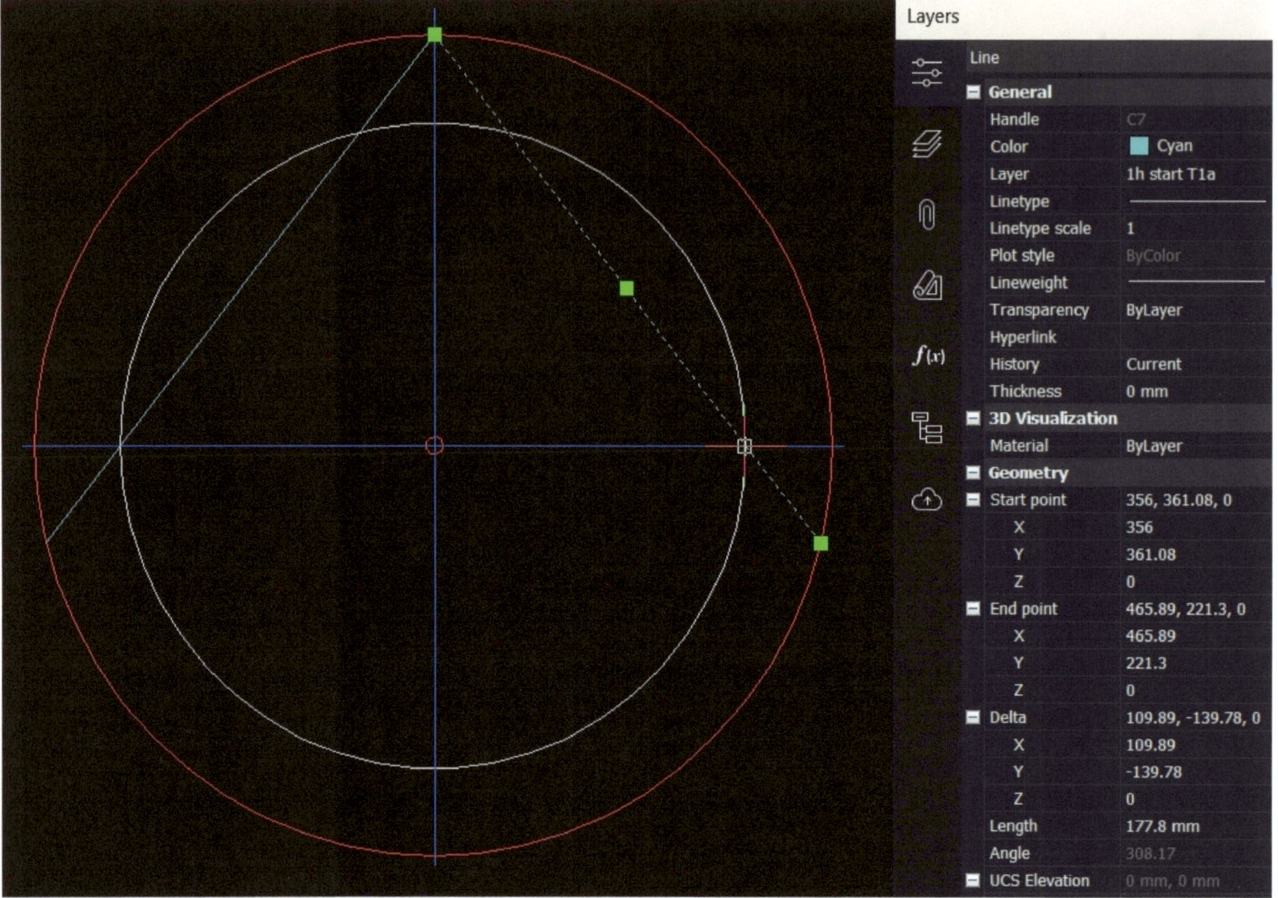

10. Draw the baseline for our Golden Ratio Triangle by simple joining the points on the red circle.

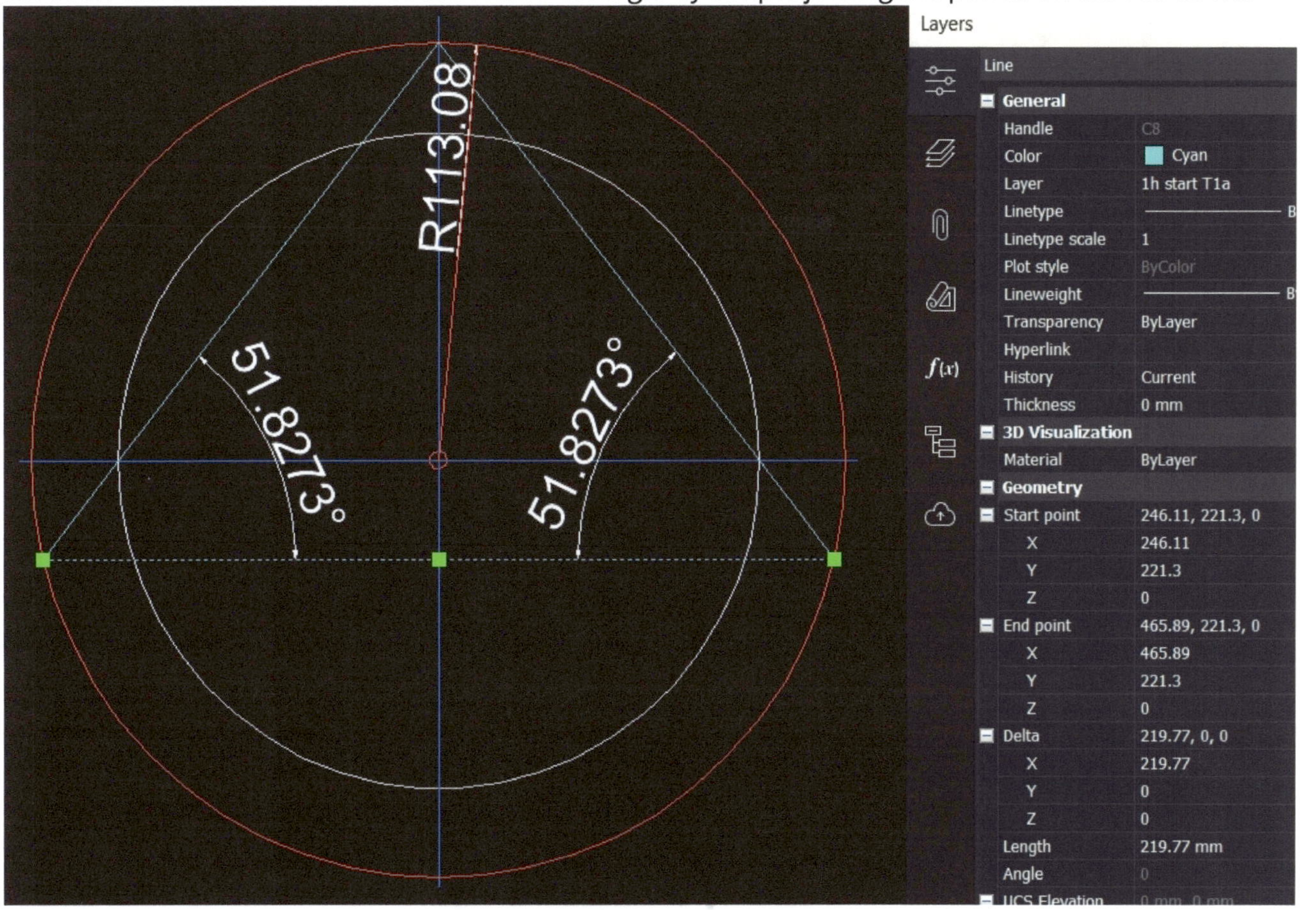

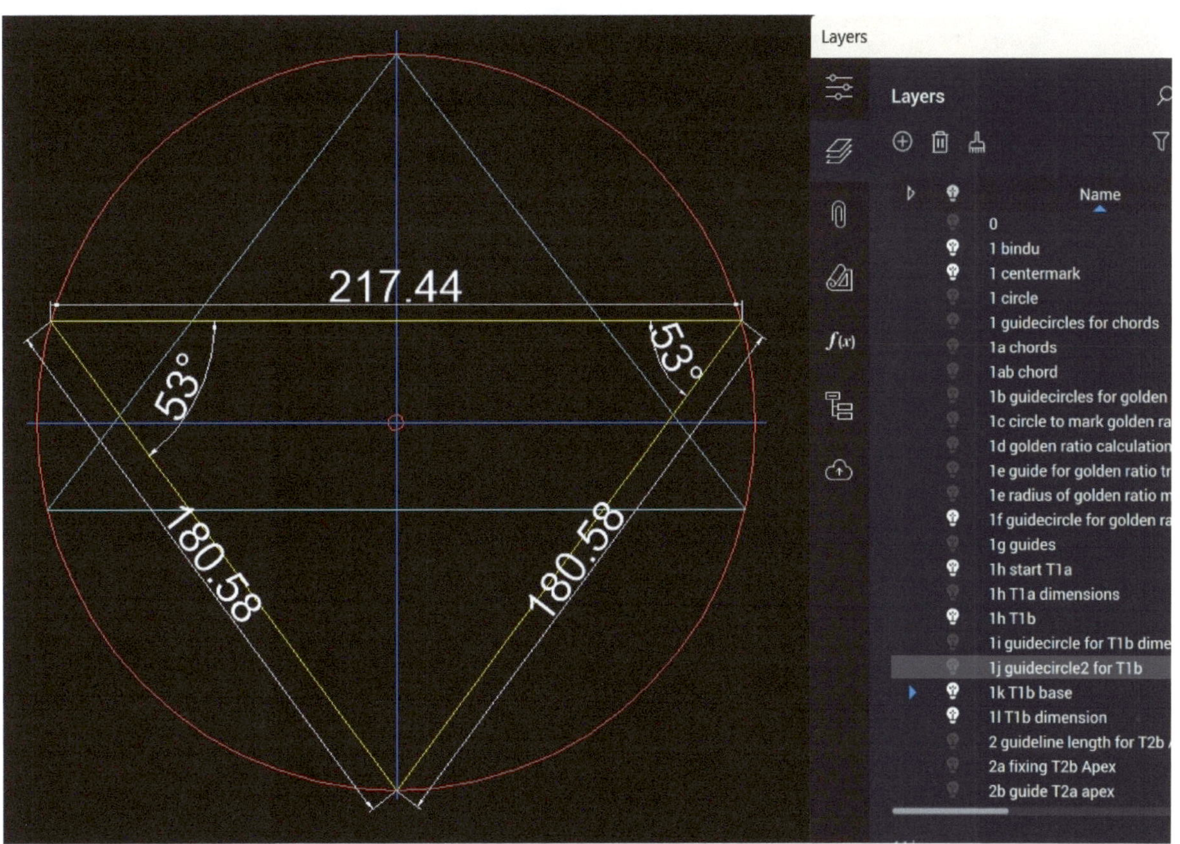

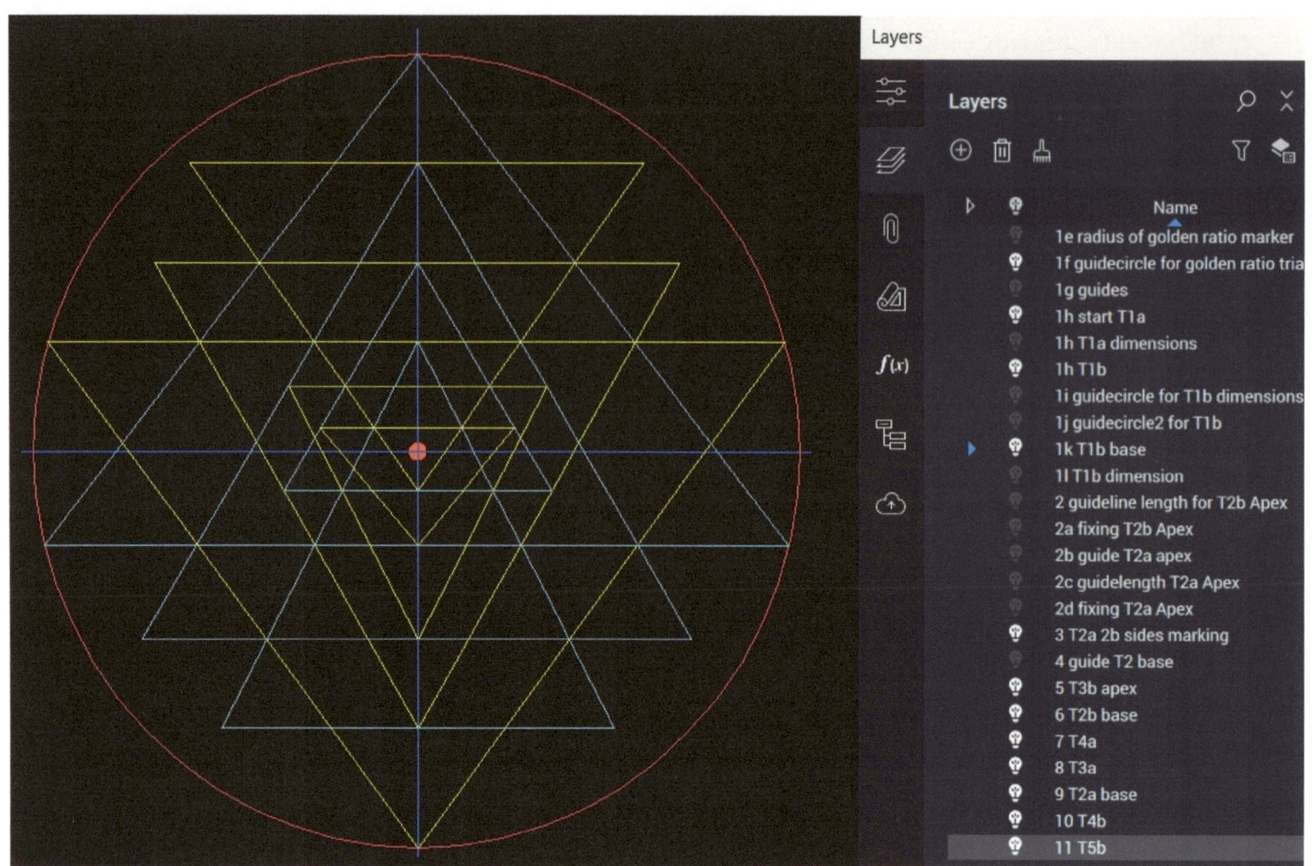

The Complete Inner 43 Triangles with Bindu of the Sri Yantra

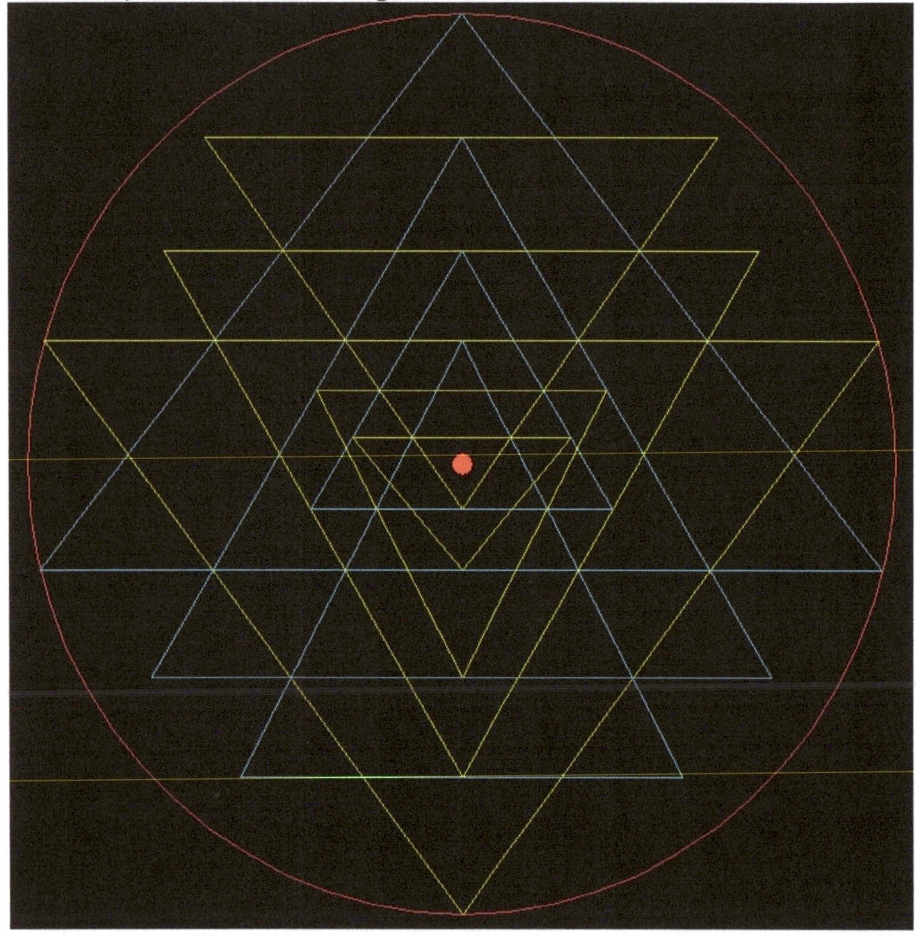

Note: On zooming to a very high magnification, we observe error in a **single Marma point only**. That is a remarkably accurate Sri Yantra!

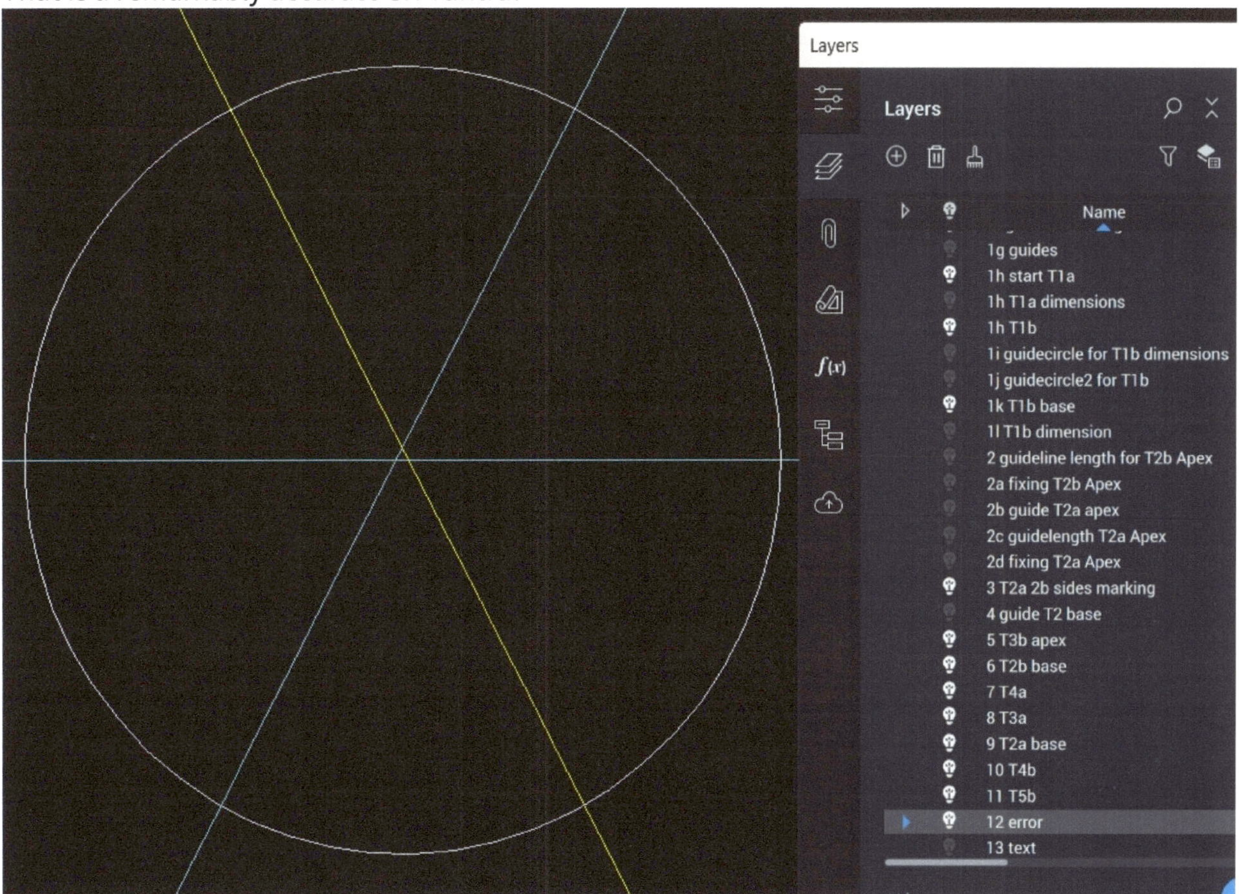

The error shown is on the Marma Node where three lines cross each other. Rest all Marma Nodes, and Sandhi Nodes are perfect!

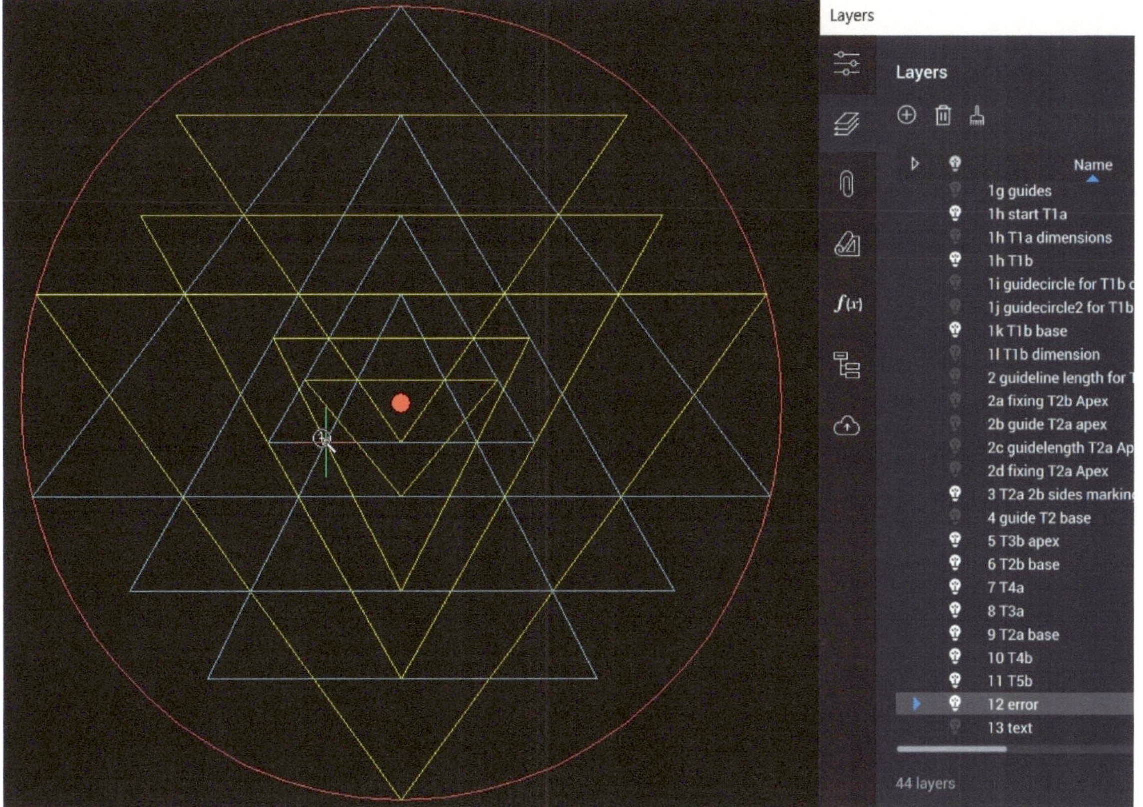

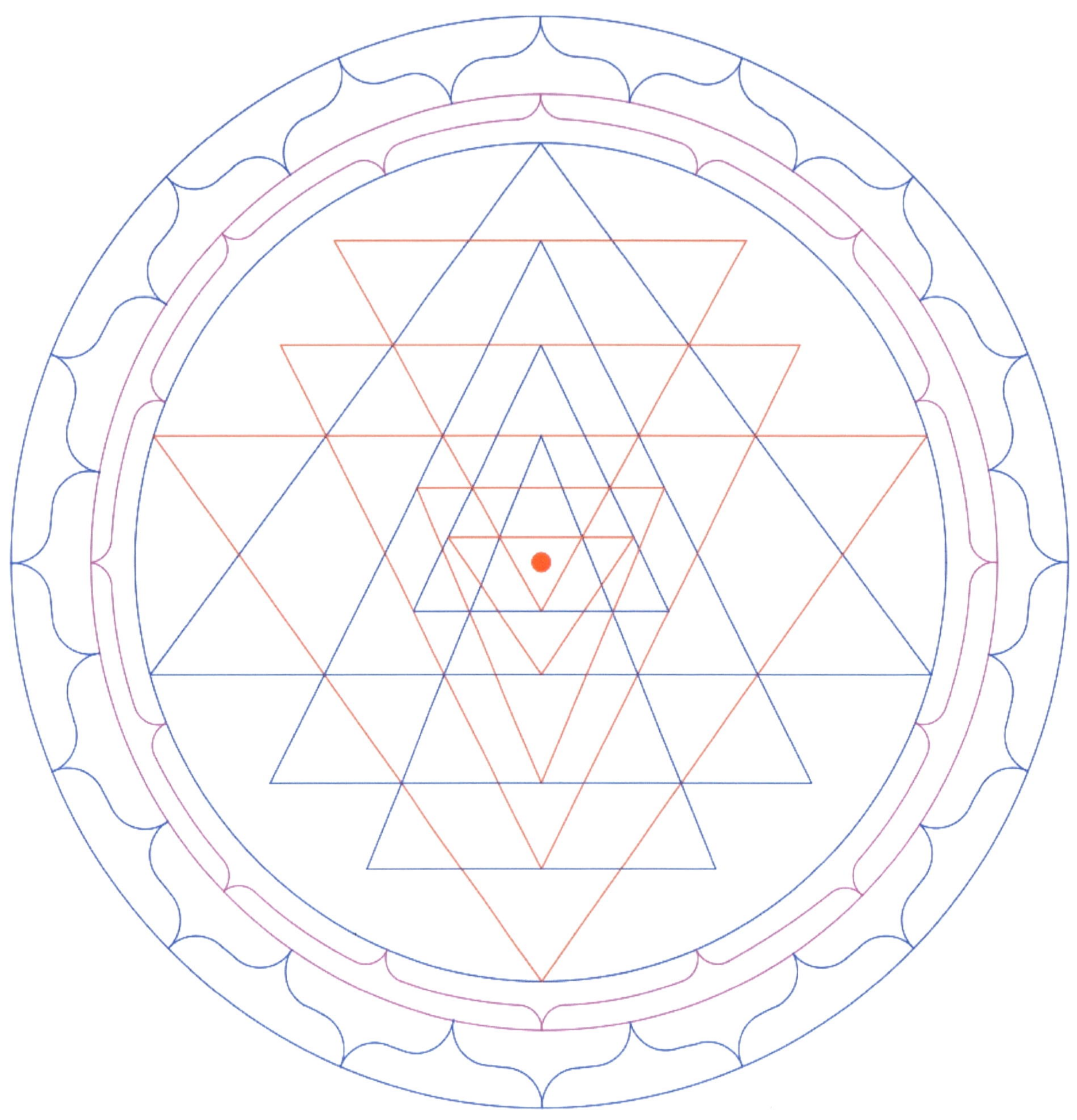

Sri Yantra without Bhupura

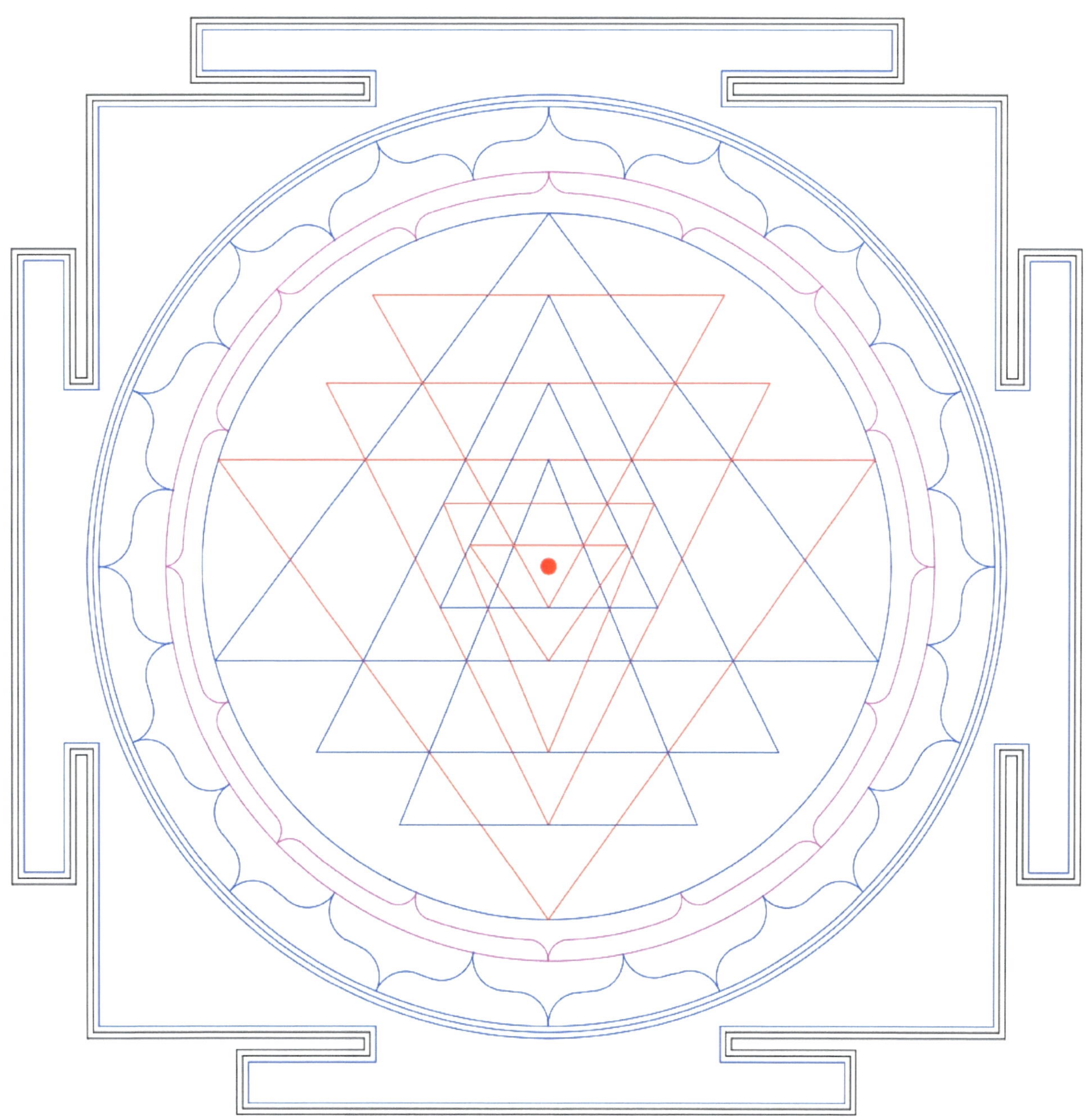

Sri Yantra with Bhupura

Latin Transliteration Chart

International Alphabet of Sanskrit Transliteration (I.A.S.T.)

a		i		u		ṛ		ḷ	
अ	आ	इ	ई	उ	ऊ	ऋ	ॠ	ऌ	
						ॢ	ॣ	ॣ	
e	ai	o	au	ṃ	m̐	ḥ	Ardha Visarga	oṃ	
ए	ऐ	ओ	औ	◌ं	◌ँ	◌:	◌ꓘ	ॐ	

Consonants shown with vowel 'a= अ' for uttering									
ka	क	ca	च	ṭa	ट	ta	त	pa	प
kha	ख	cha	छ	ṭha	ठ	tha	थ	pha	फ
ga	ग	ja	ज	ḍa	ड	da	द	ba	ब
gha	घ	jha	झ	ḍha	ढ	dha	ध	bha	भ
ṅa	ङ	ña	ञ	ṇa	ण	na	न	ma	म
ya	ra	la	va			ḻa	'		
य	र	ल	व			ळ	ऽ		
				Consonant only					
śa	ṣa	sa	ha			ka	क्अ = क		
श	ष	स	ह			k	क्		

The symbol ꓘ is pronounced as गुं guṃ. It is an ayogavaha अयोगवाह sound seen in Vedic literature due to Sandhi.

Sanskrit Alphabet and Principles in Creation

The Sanskrit Alphabet

SN	Unicode of Transliterated text	Latin	Devanagari	Remarks
1	0061	a	अ	Short vowel ह्रस्व स्वर time duration 1 units
2	0101	ā	आ	Long vowel दीर्घ स्वर time duration 2 units
3	0069	i	इ	Short vowel ह्रस्व स्वर time duration 1 units
4	012B	ī	ई	Long vowel दीर्घ स्वर time duration 2 units
5	0075	u	उ	Short vowel ह्रस्व स्वर time duration 1 units
6	016B	ū	ऊ	Long vowel दीर्घ स्वर time duration 2 units
7	1E5B	ṛ	ऋ	Short vowel ह्रस्व स्वर time duration 1 units
8	1E5D	ṝ	ॠ	Long vowel दीर्घ स्वर time duration 2 units
9	1E37	ḷ	ऌ	Short vowel ह्रस्व स्वर time duration 1 units
10	0065	e	ए	(Diphthong) Compound vowel सन्धि अक्षर duration 2
11	0061+0069	ai	ऐ	(Diphthong) Compound vowel सन्धि अक्षर duration 2
12	006F	o	ओ	(Diphthong) Compound vowel सन्धि अक्षर duration 2
13	0061+0075	au	औ	(Diphthong) Compound vowel सन्धि अक्षर duration 2
14	0061+1E43	aṃ	अं (अ ◌ं)	Ayogavaha अयोगवाह having characteristics of vowel and consonant both (अम्)
15	0061+1E25	aḥ	अः (अ ◌ः)	Ayogavaha अयोगवाह having characteristics of vowel and consonant both (अह्)
16	006B	k	क्	Consonant व्यञ्जन time duration ½ unit
17	006B+0068	kh	ख्	Consonant व्यञ्जन time duration ½ unit
18	0067	g	ग्	Consonant व्यञ्जन time duration ½ unit
19	0067+0068	gh	घ्	Consonant व्यञ्जन time duration ½ unit
20	1E45	ṅ	ङ्	Consonant व्यञ्जन time duration ½ unit
21	0063	c	च्	Consonant व्यञ्जन time duration ½ unit
22	0063+0068	ch	छ्	Consonant व्यञ्जन time duration ½ unit
23	006A	j	ज्	Consonant व्यञ्जन time duration ½ unit
24	006A+0068	jh	झ्	Consonant व्यञ्जन time duration ½ unit
25	00F1	ñ	ञ्	Consonant व्यञ्जन time duration ½ unit
26	1E6D	ṭ	ट्	Consonant व्यञ्जन time duration ½ unit
27	1E6D+0068	ṭh	ठ्	Consonant व्यञ्जन time duration ½ unit

#	Unicode	Translit.	Devanagari	Description
28	1E0D	ḍ	ड्	Consonant व्यञ्जन time duration ½ unit
29	1E0D+0068	ḍh	ढ्	Consonant व्यञ्जन time duration ½ unit
30	1E47	ṇ	ण्	Consonant व्यञ्जन time duration ½ unit
31	0074	t	त्	Consonant व्यञ्जन time duration ½ unit
32	0074+0068	th	थ्	Consonant व्यञ्जन time duration ½ unit
33	0064	d	द्	Consonant व्यञ्जन time duration ½ unit
34	0064+0068	dh	ध्	Consonant व्यञ्जन time duration ½ unit
35	006E	n	न्	Consonant व्यञ्जन time duration ½ unit
36	0070	p	प्	Consonant व्यञ्जन time duration ½ unit
37	0070+0068	ph	फ्	Consonant व्यञ्जन time duration ½ unit
38	0062	b	ब्	Consonant व्यञ्जन time duration ½ unit
39	0062+0068	bh	भ्	Consonant व्यञ्जन time duration ½ unit
40	006D	m	म्	Consonant व्यञ्जन time duration ½ unit
41	0079	y	य्	Consonant व्यञ्जन time duration ½ unit
42	0072	r	र्	Consonant व्यञ्जन time duration ½ unit
43	006C	l	ल्	Consonant व्यञ्जन time duration ½ unit
44	0076	v	व्	Consonant व्यञ्जन time duration ½ unit
45	015B	ś	श्	Consonant व्यञ्जन time duration ½ unit
46	1E63	ṣ	ष्	Consonant व्यञ्जन time duration ½ unit
47	0073	s	स्	Consonant व्यञ्जन time duration ½ unit
48	0068	h	ह्	Consonant व्यञ्जन time duration ½ unit
49	013C	ḷ	ळ्	Consonant व्यञ्जन time duration ½ unit
Unicode without Transliteration				
50	0905+0969	अ३	अ३	(Protracted) Pluta Vowel प्लुत time duration 3 units
51	0907+0969	इ३	इ३	(Protracted) Pluta Vowel प्लुत time duration 3 units
52	0909+0969	उ३	उ३	(Protracted) Pluta Vowel प्लुत time duration 3 units
53	090B+0969	ऋ३	ऋ३	(Protracted) Pluta Vowel प्लुत time duration 3 units
54	090C+0969	ऌ३	ऌ३	(Protracted) Pluta Vowel प्लुत time duration 3 units
55	090F+0969	ए३	ए३	(Protracted) Pluta Vowel प्लुत time duration 3 units
56	0913+0969	ओ३	ओ३	(Protracted) Pluta Vowel प्लुत time duration 3 units
Sanskrit Alphabet Extended to account for Principles in Creation				
57	1E39	ḹ	ॡ	Long Vowel दीर्घ स्वर time duration 2 units
58	006B+1E63+0061	kṣa	क्ष	Immutable Supreme Soul कूटस्थ

Unicode Character Sets in Use

Basic Latin	0020 to 007E
Latin-1 Supplement	00A0 to 00FF
Latin Extended-A	0100 to 017F
Latin Extended-B	0180 to 0217
Devanagari	0901 to 0970
Latin Extended Additional	1E00 to 1EF9

36 Principles in Creation

SN	Seed Sound	Principle
1	कं	Earth व्यञ्जन time duration ½ unit
2	खं	Water व्यञ्जन time duration ½ unit
3	गं	Fire व्यञ्जन time duration ½ unit
4	घं	Air व्यञ्जन time duration ½ unit
5	ङं	Space व्यञ्जन time duration ½ unit
6	चं	Smell व्यञ्जन the function of earth
7	छं	Taste व्यञ्जन the function of water
8	जं	Sight व्यञ्जन form the function of fire
9	झं	Touch व्यञ्जन the attribute of air
10	ञं	Sound व्यञ्जन attribute of space
11	टं	anus पायु organ of of elimination
12	ठं	penis उपस्थ organ of reproduction
13	डं	hands पाणी organ of grasping
14	ढं	feet पादौ organ of locomotion
15	णं	speech वाक् organ of sound
16	तं	nose घ्राण sense organ of smell
17	थं	tongue जिह्वा sense organ of taste
18	दं	eyes चक्षुस् sense organ of sight
19	धं	skin त्वक् sense organ of touch
20	नं	ears श्रोत्रम् sense organ of hearing
21	पं	nature प्रकृति primordial nature
22	फं	ego अहङ्कार notion of mineness
23	बं	intellect बुद्धि reasoning and decision
24	भं	mind मनस् controller of senses and thought producer

25	मं	Jiva soul पुरुष individual being
26	यं	Marking कला raw unprocessed touch
27	रं	Information अल्पज्ञता raw unprocessed sight
28	लं	Attachment राग raw unprocessed smell
29	वं	Time काल raw unprocessed flow
30	ळं	Event नियति raw unprocessed emptiness
31	शं	Purity शुद्ध विद्या divine expression
32	षं	Force ईश्वर raw strength
33	सं	Eternal Force सदाशिव
34	हं	Shakti शक्ति universal power and energy
35	क्षं	Shiva शिव that which holds power and energy
36	अं	Spark ब्रह्मन् that enables each and all

References

https://www.ashtangayoga.info/philosophy/sanskrit-and-devanagari/transliteration-tool/
https://www.learnsanskrit.cc/
http://www.socialresearchfoundation.com/upoadreserchpapers/3/179/1711060948461st%20vikram%20jeet%20%20final.pdf
https://srilalithatripurasundari.wordpress.com/an-analysis-on-the-correlation-of-great-goddess-sri-lalita-devi-and-the-sri-cakra-2/
https://bhaskaraprakasha.org/publications/text

Bhavanopanishad Chant and explanation https://www.youtube.com/watch?v=zHLQP6mogB4

Draw the Sri Yantra (Patrick Flanagan)
https://sriyantraresearch.com/Construction/Flanagan/patrick_flanagan_method.htm

Draw the Sri Yantra by George Leoniak
https://knewgeometry.space/   https://www.youtube.com/watch?v=wqvYPCBEWWs

Draw the Sri Yantra by Zak Korvin
https://circle.gtryp.com/circle/tutorial-sri-yantra-version-1/   https://zkorvin.com/

Antonio Alessi https://pi-day.eye-of-revelation.org/Square-From-Circle.html#ratioceleste
Srimadh Lalita Maha Tripurasundari Devasthanam http://www.slmt.co.in/Home/Navaavaranam

S. Subhramanya Sastri, T. R. Srinivasa Ayyangar –Saundarya Lahiri - 1st – 1948 – The Theosophical Publishing House, Adyar, Madras.

S. K. Ramachandra Rao – The Tantra of Sri Chakra (Bhavanopanishat) - 1st – 1983 –Sharada Prakashana, Bangalore.

Rajendra Ranjan Chaturvedi – श्रीविद्या कल्पलता - 1st – 1998 – Motilal Banarsidass, Delhi.

Sri Sivananda, Krishnanand Budhauliya – श्रीमातृकाचक्र विवेकः – 2nd – 1998 – Sripitambara Pitha Sanskrit Parishad, Datia, Madhya Pradesh.

Sri Karapatra Swami, Sri Sitarama Kaviraja – श्रीविद्यारत्नाकरः - 8th – 2012 – Srividya Sadhana Pitha, Varanasi.

V. Ravi – Understanding and Worshipping Sri Chakra - 1st – 2013 – Manblunder Publication, Chennai.

Ashwini Kumar Aggarwal – Maheshwar Sutras Pratyaharas – 1st – 2018 –
                    – The Sanskrit Alphabet with Vedic Extensions – 1st – 2021 –
Devotees of Sri Sri Ravi Shankar Ashram, Punjab.

When one stops still and listens, a sound is heard. Felt within.

Perhaps it is that Om, the un-struck without origin.

सर्वे भवन्तु सुखिनः । सर्वे सन्तु निरामयाः ।

सर्वे भद्राणि पश्यन्तु । मा कश्चिद् दुःख भाग् भवेत् ॥

ॐ शान्तिः शान्तिः शान्तिः ॥

When faith has blossomed in life, Every step is led by the Divine.

Sri Sri Ravi Shankar

Om Namah Shivaya

जय गुरुदेव